Study Guide Part 2: Chapters 8-10

To Accompany

# Accounting Principles

## Fourth Canadian Edition

**JERRY J. WEYGANDT** *Ph.D., C.P.A.*

Arthur Andersen Alumni Professor of Accounting
University of Wisconsin – Madison
Madison, Wisconsin

**DONALD E. KIESO** *Ph.D., C.P.A.*

KPMG Peat Marwick Emeritus Professor of Accountancy
North Illinois University
DeKalb, Illinois

**PAUL D. KIMMEL** *Ph.D., C.P.A.*

University of Wisconsin – Milwaukee
North Illinois University
Milwaukee, Wisconsin

**BARBARA TRENHOLM** *M.B.A., F.C.A.*

University of New Brunswick
Fredericton, New Brunswick

**VALERIE A. KINNEAR** *M.Sc. (Bus. Admin.), C.A.*

Mount Royal College
Calgary, Alberta

*Prepared by*
**CAROLE REID CLYNE** *C.M.A., M.Ed.*

Centennial College
Toronto, Ontario

**JOHN WILEY AND SONS CANADA, LTD**

**Library and Archives Canada Cataloguing in Publication**

Reid Clyne, Carole
      Study guide to accompany Accounting principles, fourth Canadian edition, Jerry J. Weygandt ... [et al.] / Carole Reid Clyne.

Supplement to:  Accounting principles.

ISBN 978-0-470-83947-8 (pt. 1).—ISBN 978-0-470-83948-5 (pt. 2)

1.  Accounting—Problems, exercises, etc.  I.  Title.

HF5635.A3778 2006 Suppl. 1      657'.044      C2007-900433-4

**Production Credits**

Editorial Manager: Karen Staudinger
Publishing Services Director: Karen Bryan
Editorial Assistant: Sara Dam
Director of Marketing: Isabelle Moreau
Cover Design: Interrobang Graphic Design
Printing & Binding: Webcom Inc.

Printed and bound in Canada
1 2 3 4 5 WC 11 10 09 08 07

John Wiley & Sons Canada Ltd.
6045 Freemont Blvd
Mississauga, ON
L5R 4J3
Visit our website at: www.wiley.ca

# CONTENTS PART 2

# TO THE STUDENT

This study guide will aid you significantly in your study of Accounting Principles, Fourth Canadian Edition, by Jerry J. Weygandt, Donald E. Kieso, Paul D. Kimmel, Barbara Trenholm and Valerie Kinnear. The material in the study guide is designed to reinforce your understanding of the principles and procedures presented in the textbook. It is important to recognize that the study guide is a supplement to and not a substitute for the textbook.

This study guide contains the following materials for each chapter in the textbook:

- Study objectives
- Preview of the chapter
- Chapter review of key points
- Demonstration problem and solution
- Multiple choice questions
- Matching exercise for key terms and definitions
- Exercises

Solutions to the review questions and exercises are provided at the end of each chapter to help you assess how well you understand the material. The solutions explain the reasoning behind the answer, so you get immediate feedback as to what, how, and why.

To benefit the most from this study guide, we recommend you take the following steps:

1. Carefully read the chapter material in the textbook.
2. Read the chapter preview and review in the study guide.
3. Take notes in class.
4. Answer the questions and exercises for the chapter in the study guide and compare your answers with the solutions provided. If you answer a question incorrectly, refer back to the textbook for a discussion of the point you missed.
5. Solve the end-of-chapter material in the textbook as assigned by your instructor.

**The study guide should help you prepare for examinations**. The chapter review points, class notes, and other materials will help you determine how well you can recall information presented in each chapter. When you have identified topics that you need to study further, return to the textbook for a complete discussion.

In addition to this study guide, the following supplementary materials are available from your bookstore or the publisher for use with the textbook Accounting Principles, Fourth Canadian Edition.

# Special Student Supplements That Help You Get The Best Grade You Can

## The Accounting Principles Resource Website

This site serves as a launching pad to numerous activities and resources for all students. You will find a series of study aids and practice tools: animated tutorials to help with key accounting concepts; interactive quizzes, an online glossary, and additional demonstration problems to help prepare for class and tests; and a comprehensive section on ethics in accounting. In addition, there are links to companies discussed in the text, downloadable resources such as a checklist of key figures and PowerPoint presentations, and much more.

www.wiley.com/canada/weygandt

## WileyPLUS

Your instructor may be using *WileyPLUS*, an online suite of resources that includes a complete multi-media version of the text that will help you come to class better prepared for lectures, and allows you to track your progress throughout the course more easily. If so, you have access to a complete e-book with links to tools such as self-assessment quizzes and animated tutorials to help you study more efficiently. *WileyPLUS* is designed to provide instant feedback as you practise on your own. You can work through assignments with automatic grading or review custom-made class presentations featuring reading assignments, PowerPoint slides, and interactive simulations.

## Working Papers

Working Papers are partially completed accounting forms for the end-of-chapter brief exercises, exercises, and problems. Journals, ledgers, T accounts, and other required working papers have been predetermined and included for each textbook assignment, so that you can redirect limited time to important accounting concepts rather than formatting.

## City Cycle Practice Set

This practice set exposes you to a real-world simulation of maintaining a complete set of accounting records for a business. Business papers add a realistic dimension by enabling you to handle documents, cheques, invoices, and receipts that you would encounter in a small proprietorship. This practice set reinforces key concepts from Chapters 1 through 4 and allows you to apply the information you have learned. It is an excellent way to see how these concepts are all brought together to generate the accounting information that is essential in assessing the financial position and operating results of a company.

## Suggestions for Effective Studying

Want to get better grades? Read on!

Good students have a system for studying. In the next few pages, we'll give you some guidelines that we think can help improve the way you study—not only in your accounting principles course, but in every course. If you need more specific help, we suggest you ask your instructor or consult a career counsellor at your school.

## How to Use a Textbook

Textbooks often include material designed to help you study. It's worth your while to flip through a textbook and look for:

- **The Preface**. If an author has a point of view, you can find it here, along with notes on how the book is meant to be used.
- **The Table of Contents**. Reading the table of contents will help you understand how the topics covered in the book fit together.
- **Glossary**. The most important terms and ideas for you to know will be in the glossary, either at the end of each chapter or at the end of the book.
- **Appendices**. Found at the end of certain chapters, appendices contain such things as:
  - More difficult material.
  - Answers to selected problems.
  - Specimen financial statements.

## How to Read a Chapter

Before Class: Skim

Unless you're told to know a chapter thoroughly by class time, it's a good idea just to skim it before class.

- Become familiar with the main ideas so that the lecture will make more sense to you.
- As you skim, ask yourself if you know something about the material.
- Keep any questions you have in mind for the lecture, so that you can listen for the answers.

In particular, look for:

- **Study Objectives**. These are what you will be expected to know—and be able to do or explain—by the end of the chapter.
- **Chapter-Opening Vignettes**. Each chapter opens with a brief story that reflects the topic of the chapter. The story or "vignette" will give you an idea of how accounting relates to your day-to-day life.
- **Boldface or *Italic* Terms**. These are important terms, concepts, or people.
- **Headings**. Read the major headings to see how the material fits together. How are the ideas related to each other? Do they make sense to you?
- **Summary**. A good summary repeats the main points and conclusions of the chapter, but it does not explain them. The summary usually matches up with the study objectives and introduction to the chapter.

# After Class: Read

After skimming the chapter and attending class, you are ready to read the chapter in more detail.

- **Check for Meaning**. Ask yourself as you read if you understand what the material means.
- **Don't Skip the Tables, Figures, and Illustrations**. They contain important information that may be on a test. They may also offer a different perspective on the material and help to deepen your understanding of it.
- **Read the Sidebars and Feature Boxes**. These items are set off from the main text, either in the margin or in colour boxes. They may include real-world examples, amusing anecdotes, or additional material.
- **Review**. Read the chapter again, especially the parts you found difficult. Review the study objectives, chapter introduction, summary, and key terms to make sure you understand them.
- **End-of-Chapter Questions**. Do all the end-of-chapter questions, exercises, or problems. For the exercises and problems, make sure you have memorized which equations or rules apply and why. Do any practice problems assigned by your instructor, too. These problems will not only help you, but show you what kind of questions might be on a test. If you have trouble with any:
  - Review the part of the chapter that applies.
  - Look for similar questions and do them.
  - Ask yourself which concept or equation should be applied.
- **Use the Study Guide**. After you've read and studied the chapter, use the study guide to identify which areas you need to review in the text.

# How to Take Notes

The ability to take notes is a skill, and one you can learn. First, a few practical tips:

- Arrive in class on time and don't leave early. You might miss important notes or assignments.
- Sit close enough to the instructor so you can hear him or her and read overhead transparencies.
- If you don't understand, ask questions.
- Do not read the text during class—you'll miss what the instructor is saying. Listen, take notes, and ask questions.

Now for the note-taking itself:

- **Listen for Ideas**. Don't try to write everything the instructor says. Instead, listen and take notes on the main ideas and any supporting ideas and examples. Make sure you include names, dates, and new terms. In accounting classes, take down all rules, equations, and theories, as well as every step in a demonstration problem.
- **Use Outlines**. Organize ideas into outlines. Indent supporting ideas under the main ones.
- **Abbreviate**. To help you write more quickly, use abbreviations, either standard ones or ones you make up. For example, leaving out vowels can sometimes help: Lvg out vwls can ...).
- **Leave Space**. Leave enough space in your notes so that you can add material if the instructor goes back to the topic or expands a problem later.

# How to Use a Study Guide (In General)

A study guide is specific to the textbook you use. It can't replace the text; it can only point out places where you need more work. To use a study guide effectively:

- Use it only after you've read the chapter and reviewed your class notes.
- Ask yourself if you really understand the chapter's main points and how they relate to each other.
- Go back and reread the sections of your text that deal with any questions you missed. The text will not ask the same questions as the study guide, but it can help you to understand the material better. If that doesn't work, ask your instructor for help.
- Remember that a study guide can't cover any extra material that your instructor may lecture on in class.

# How to Take Tests

Studying for a Test

Studying for tests is a process that starts with the first class and ends only with the last test. All through the semester, it helps to:

- Follow the advice we gave about reading a chapter and taking notes.
- Review your notes:
    - immediately after class. Clear up anything you can't read and circle important items while the lecture is still fresh in your mind.
    - periodically during the semester.
    - before a test.
- Use videotapes of lectures, if they have been made.

Now you're ready to do your final studying for a test. Leave as much time as you need, and study under the conditions that are right for you—alone or with a study group, in the library or another quiet place. It helps to schedule several short study sessions rather than to study all at one time.

- **Reread the chapter(s)**. Follow this system:
    - Most importantly, look for things you don't remember or don't understand.
    - Reinforce your understanding of the main ideas by rereading the introduction, study objectives, and summary.
    - Read the chapter from beginning to end.
- **Redo the problems**. Make sure you know which equation to apply or procedure to follow in different situations and why.
- **Test Yourself**. Cover up something you've just read and try to explain it to yourself—or to a friend—out loud.
- **Use Memory Tricks**. If you're having trouble remembering something—such as a formula or items in a list—try associating it with something you know or make a sentence out of the first letters.
- **Study with a Group**. Group study is helpful after you've done all your own studying. You can help each other with problems and by quizzing each other, but you'll probably just distract each other if you try to review a chapter together.

(**A Note about Cramming. Don't!** If you cram, you will probably only remember what you've read for a short time, and you'll have trouble knowing how to generalize from it. If you must cram, concentrate on the main ideas, the supporting ideas, main headings, boldface or italicized items, and study objectives.)

## Taking a Test

After giving you some general tips, we'll focus on different types of tests: objective, problem, and essay.

- **Before the Test**

  - Make sure you eat well and get enough sleep.
  - If the instructor doesn't say in class what material will be covered or what kind of test it will be, ask.
  - Arrive early enough to get settled.
  - Bring everything you need—bluebook, pens, pencils, eraser, calculator—and the book, if it's an open-book test!

- **As You Begin the Test**

  - Read the instructions completely. Do you have to answer all of the questions? Do certain questions apply to others? Do some questions count more than others? Will incorrect answers be counted against you? \
  - Schedule your time. How many questions are there? Try to estimate how much time to leave for each section. If sections are timed so that you won't be able to return to them, make sure you leave enough time to decide which questions to answer.

- **Taking the Test**

  - Read each question completely as you come to it.
  - Answer the easier questions first and go back to the harder ones.
  - Concentrate on questions that count more.
  - Jot notes or equations in the margin if you think it will help.
  - Review your answers and don't change an answer unless you're sure it's wrong.

- **Dealing with Panic**

  - Relax. Do this by tightening and relaxing one muscle at a time.
  - Breathe deeply.
  - If you don't know an answer, go on to the next question.

## Objective Tests
## (Multiple choice, true-false, matching, completion or fill-in-the blanks)

- Watch out for words such as "always," "all," "every," "none," or "never." Very few things are always or never so. If a question or answer includes these words, be careful.
- If you are uncertain about a multiple choice answer, try to narrow the choices down to two and make an educated guess.
- On a matching test, match up the easy ones first. This will leave fewer possibilities for the hard ones.
- Make educated guesses for objective questions. If you really have no idea and a wrong answer will count against you, leave it blank.

## Problem Tests

- If an equation is long, jot it down before you work on the problem.
- Remember that math builds one equation on another. If you can't remember a particular equation, try to remember how it was derived.
- Don't despair if you can't figure out what a question is calling for. Try to figure out part of it first. If that doesn't work, go on; sometimes a later question will jog your memory.
- If your instructor gives credit for partially correct problems, make sure you include the way you worked out a problem.
- Make sure that your calculator works before the test and, just in case, know how to do the problems without it. Sometimes you can hit the wrong button, so it helps to have a rough idea of what your calculator should be giving you.

## Essay Tests

- Write a rough outline before you begin. If that takes too much time, just jot down all the things you want to say and then number them. Organize what you're going to say into groups of related ideas.
- Make a point in each paragraph. The easiest way is to make the point in the paragraph's first sentence and then back it up.
- Use examples, facts, and dates to back up what you are saying.
- Do what the question asks for. If it asks you to compare two things, for example, go back and forth between them; don't spend all your time on one of them.
- If you have no idea what to write, try to remember ideas that your instructor stressed in class and see if you can relate the question to those ideas.
- Check your time. If you're running out, write your last points down without explaining them; your teacher will at least know what you were going to explain.

# chapter 8
# Accounting for Receivables

## study objectives >>

After studying this chapter, you should be able to:

1. Record accounts receivable transactions.
2. Calculate the net realizable value of accounts receivable and account for bad debts.
3. Account for notes receivable.
4. Demonstrate the presentation, analysis, and management of receivables.

# Preview of Chapter 8

In this chapter we will review the journal entries made when goods and services are sold on account and when cash is collected from those sales. In addition, the chapter covers how companies estimate, record, and, in some cases, collect accounts that were previously uncollectible. We will also learn about notes receivable.

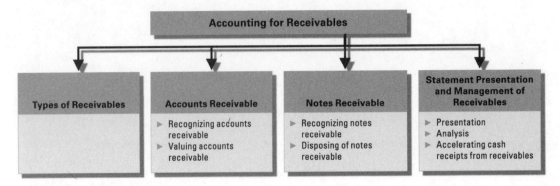

# Types of Receivables

Receivables are claims that are expected to be collected in cash. They are usually due from individuals and other companies. The two most common types of receivables are accounts receivable and notes receivable.

**Accounts receivable** are amounts owed by customers on account. They result from sales of goods and services. **Notes receivable** are claims for which formal instruments of credit are issued as proof of debt. Notes and accounts receivable that result from sale transactions are also called trade receivables.

# Accounts Receivable

**study objective 1**

**Record accounts receivable transactions.**

Two important accounting issues for accounts receivable are recognizing accounts receivable and valuing accounts receivable. Disposing of accounts receivable will be covered later in the chapter.

## Recognizing Accounts Receivable

Accounts receivable are recorded when a merchandise company records the sale of merchandise or when a service company records a service provided on account. Accounts receivable are also recognized as being reduced by sales returns and allowances and sales discounts.

### Subsidiary Accounts Receivable Ledger
A business usually has several, or sometimes hundreds, of customers. If it recorded the dollar amounts owed by each customer in the one general ledger account, Accounts Receivable, it would be difficult to determine the balance owed by any one customer at a specific time. To keep track of each customer, companies use a **subsidiary ledger** for each one.

Each entry affecting accounts receivable is basically posted twice: once to the general ledger and once to the subsidiary ledger. Entries to the subsidiary ledger are posted daily, while entries to the general ledger are summarized and posted monthly.

The accounts receivable general ledger account is now the **control account**. The balance of the control account must agree with the total of the balances in the individual accounts receivable in the subsidiary ledger at all times. (See Illustration 8-1 of text.)

### Interest Revenue

At the end of each month, the company can use the subsidiary ledger to easily determine the transactions that occurred in each customer's account during the month. They may send the customer a statement of transactions for the month. If the customer does not pay in full within a specified time, most retailers add interest charges to the balance due.

Finance charges added to an account must be recognized on the seller's books as interest revenue. Interest revenue, when charged to customers on overdue accounts, is included in other revenues in the non-operating section of the income statement. Interest revenue is recorded as an increase to accounts receivable, as follows:

| Accounts Receivable | XXX | |
| Sales | | XXX |

### Non-bank Credit Card Sales

Debit and bank credit card sales are cash sales.  Sales on credit cards that are not directly associated with a bank are reported as credit sales.  For example, sales using company credit cards such as Canadian Tire are always recorded as credit sales by the company.  The amount is receivable from the customer who uses the company's credit card.  If that customer had used a bank credit card, the amount would have been recorded as a cash sale by the company.

Transactions and payments can now be processed much more quickly in the electronic environment. If it takes longer than a day or two to process the non-bank credit card transaction and collect cash, it should be treated like a credit sale.

## Valuing Accounts Receivable

Receivables should be reported on the balance sheet as a current asset. Reporting is sometimes difficult because not all receivables will be collected. The net realizable value is the amount of the receivables that will be collected. Net realizable value is the amount that should be reported in the financial statements.

study objective 2

Calculate the net realizable value of accounts receivable and account for bad debts.

When receivables are written down to their net realizable value because of credit losses, owner's equity must also be reduced. This is done by recording an expense, known as bad debts expense, for the credit losses. If a company waits until it knows the specific accounts that will not be collected, it would end up recording the bad debts expense long after the revenue is recorded.

To record bad debts in the period in which the revenue occurs, the company must estimate the uncollectible accounts receivable. The **allowance method** is used to estimate uncollectible accounts and match expected credit losses against sales in the accounting period in which the sales occur.

The allowance method is required for financial reporting purposes when the amount of bad debts is significant. Its three essential features are:
1. **Recording estimated uncollectibles:** Uncollectible accounts receivable (expenses) are estimated and recorded against revenues in the accounting period in which the revenues occurred.
2. **Recording the write off of an uncollectible account:** Actual uncollectible accounts are written off at the time each specific account is determined to be uncollectible.
3. **Recovery of an uncollectible account:** When an account that was previously written off is later collected, the original write off is reversed and collection recorded.

Neither the write off nor the later recovery affects the income statement. Matching is therefore not affected by the timing of these entries.

## 1. Recording Estimated Uncollectibles

The adjusting entry to record estimated uncollectibles is as follows:

| | | |
|---|---|---|
| Bad Debts Expense | XXX | |
| Allowance for Doubtful Accounts | | XXX |
| To record estimate of uncollectible accounts | | |

Bad Debts Expense is debited, and is reported on the income statement as an operating expense. The account credited, Allowance for Doubtful Accounts, is a contra asset account that shows the amounts that are estimated to be uncollectible in the future.

Allowance for Doubtful Accounts, a contra account to Accounts Receivable, is used instead of Accounts Receivable. With the use of the contra account, the total of the subsidiary accounts balances remains exactly equal to the control account, Accounts Receivable. Also, the estimate of the uncollectible accounts does not distort the actual amounts posted to the Accounts Receivable.

The Allowance for Doubtful Accounts, subtracted from the Accounts Receivable, gives the value of the amount of receivables expected to be received in cash. This is the Net Realizable Value and is calculated as follows:

$$\text{Accounts Receivable} - \text{Allowance for Doubtful Accounts} = \text{Net Realizable Value}$$

**Estimating the Allowance.** Companies must estimate the amount of uncollectible accounts. Two approaches may be used: (1) percentage of sales, and (2) percentage of receivables. Both approaches are acceptable, and the choice is a management decision.

**Percentage of Sales Approach.** The percentage of sales approach calculates bad debts expense as a percentage of net credit sales. Management determines the percentage based on past experience and likely credit policy.

For example, Manahan Company estimates that 5% of its $100,000 net credit sales will become uncollectible. So, the estimated bad debts expense is $5,000 (5% x $100,000). The adjusting entry to record the estimate of uncollectible accounts for the year ended 2008 is:

| | | | |
|---|---|---|---|
| Dec. 31 | Bad Debts Expense | 5,000 | |
| | Allowance for Doubtful Accounts | | 5,000 |
| | To record estimate of bad debts expense | | |

The percentage of sales approach is quick and easy to use. It is often used in estimating bad debts for interim reports. It is an excellent matching of expenses with revenues because bad debts expense is related to the sales recorded in the period.

**Percentage of Receivables Approach.** Under the percentage of receivables approach, management uses experience to estimate the percentage of receivables that will become uncollectible. The percentage may be applied to the receivables as a whole, or applied with different percentages to customer balances according to the length of time that they have remained unpaid.

This approach improves the reliability of the estimate. This method gives a better estimate of **net realizable value** of the accounts receivable.

For example, Manahan Company estimated that 10% of $500,000 receivables will become uncollectible. Before recording the estimated bad debts, the Allowance for Doubtful Accounts has a credit balance of $20,000. The estimated uncollectible accounts applied to the receivables as a whole is $50,000 (10% x $500,000). This is the required balance in the Allowance for Doubtful Accounts at the balance sheet date. The amount of the adjusting entry is the difference between the required balance ($50,000 CR) and the existing balance ($20,000 CR) in the allowance account. The adjusting entry to record the estimated uncollectible accounts for the year ended 2008 is:

        Dec. 31            Bad Debts Expense                    30,000
                                    Allowance for Doubtful Accounts        30,000
                           To record estimate of bad debts expense

If the allowance account had a debit balance prior to the adjustment, the adjusting entry would still be the difference between the required balance and the existing balance. For example, assume the Manahan Company estimated uncollectible accounts to be $50,000 and the allowance account has a debit balance of $5,000. The amount of the adjusting entry is the difference between the required balance ($50,000 CR) and the existing balance ($5,000 DR) in the allowance account. The adjusting entry to record the estimated uncollectible accounts for the year ended 2008 would be:

        Dec. 31            Bad Debts Expense                    55,000
                                    Allowance for Doubtful Accounts        55,000
                           To record estimate of bad debts expense

The percentage of receivables approach gives a better estimate of the net realizable value of the accounts receivable than does the percentage of sales approach.

## 2. Recording the Write Off of an Uncollectible Account

Companies use various methods to collect past-due accounts. When all means of collecting appear impossible, the account should be written off. To prevent premature write offs, each write off should be approved in writing by management.

For example, Manahan Company authorizes the write off of a $300 balance owed by a customer, Ascott, on February 3, 2009. The journal entry to record the write off of this uncollectible account is as follows:

        Feb. 9             Allowance for Doubtful Accounts      300
                                    Accounts Receivable—Ascott                300
                           To record write off of uncollectible account

---

**TIP**

**Bad Debts Expense is never used to record a write off** of an account. Bad debts expense is an estimate of uncollectible accounts for the current period, and is recorded at the end of the reporting period to ensure matching of expense to revenue. Remember that the bad debts expense account would be closed at the end of the period, during the closing process.

---

The write off affects only balance sheet accounts. The write off reduces both accounts receivable and the allowance for doubtful accounts by the same amount, and so the net realizable value on the balance sheet remains the same.

### 3. Recovery of an Uncollectible Account

Sometimes a customer pays an amount that a company has previously written off as uncollectible. For example, on August 15, 2009, Ascott pays the $300 amount that had been written off on February 3. The entries to record the receipt from the customer are as follows:

| | | | |
|---|---|---|---|
| Aug. 15 | Accounts Receivable—Ascott | 300 | |
| |     Allowance for Doubtful Accounts | | 300 |
| | To reverse the write off of Ascott | | |
| | | | |
| Aug. 15 | Cash | 300 | |
| |     Accounts Receivable—Ascott | | 300 |
| | To record collection from Ascott | | |

When the entries are posted to the General Ledger control account, the customer's account in the subsidiary ledger must also be updated. This would update the customer's activity with the company and help when credit is being considered in the future.

### Summary of Allowance Method

Three types of transactions may be used when valuing accounts receivable using the allowance method:

1. Uncollectible accounts receivable, determined by using either the percentage of sales approach or the percentage of receivables approach, are recorded by debiting Bad Debts Expense and crediting Allowance for Doubtful Accounts.
2. Write offs of actual uncollectible accounts are debited to Allowance for Doubtful Accounts and credited to Accounts Receivable in the next accounting period.
3. Amounts recovered, if any, after write offs require two journal entries to restore the customer history and to record the receipt of the account. This helps when considering future customer credit.

# Notes Receivable

A note receivable is a written promise to pay an amount owed, which gives the payee a legal claim. It differs from an account receivable, which is an informal promise to pay. The note is a negotiable instrument (similar to a cheque) and it can be transferred to another party when endorsed or signed by the payee.

Credit may also be granted in exchange for a formal credit instrument known as a promissory note. A promissory note is a written promise to pay a specified amount of money on demand or at a definite time. The party making the promise is called the maker; the party to whom payment is made is called the payee. Credit may be granted in exchange for a promissory note.

The promissory note, identifying the payee by name or simply as the bearer, is a note receivable. The note details the names of the parties, the amount of the loan, the loan period, the interest rate, and the note due date, and gives the payee a stronger legal claim to the borrower's assets.

The basic issues for notes receivable are similar to those of accounts receivable:

1. Recognizing notes receivable
2. Disposing of notes receivable

## Recognizing Notes Receivable

A note receivable may be exchanged for an accounts receivable. For example, the Alba Company accepts a $9,000 note receivable from Tross Ltd. in settlement of an accounts receivable. The note has an interest rate of 5% per year and is due in six months on December 31. The entry to record the transaction is as follows:

    July 1                  Note Receivable—Tross Ltd.        9,000
                                 Accounts Receivable—Tross Ltd.        9,000
                            To record acceptance of the Tross note

When a note is exchanged for an account receivable, the customer might have had several invoices not paid within a given 30-day period. The exchange, in settlement of this open account, would give the company a stronger legal claim on the funds owed by the customer.

### Recording Interest

The interest rate specified on the note is always the rate of interest for one year (annual rate). Interest is calculated by applying the annual rate of interest to the note's face value, and then dividing the amount calculated by the number of months from date of issue to date of maturity.

The basic formula for calculating interest on an interest-bearing note is:

| Face Value of Note | x | Annual Interest Rate | x | Time in Terms of One Year | = | Interest |
|---|---|---|---|---|---|---|
| $9,000 | x | 5% | x | 6/12 | = | $225 |

The Alba Company journal entry to record the interest owed for the month of July is:

    July 31                 Interest Receivable                    37.50
                                 Interest Revenue ($9,000 x 5% x 1/12)  37.50
                            To accrue interest on the Tross note receivable

Interest on the note receivable is recorded in a separate account. The note is a formal credit instrument and its recorded value stays at its face value.

### Valuing Notes Receivable

Like accounts receivable, notes receivable are reported at their net realizable value. Each note must be analyzed to determine how likely it is to be collected, similar to those for Accounts Receivable. If eventual collection is doubtful, a bad debts expense and an allowance for doubtful notes must be recorded. Some companies use only one allowance account for both accounts and notes receivable. It is the Allowance for Doubtful Accounts.

## Disposing of Notes Receivable

Notes Receivable are held to their maturity when interest and any unpaid interest is due. This is known as honouring (paying) the note. If the maker of the note does not pay the amount owing at maturity, adjustments must be made to the accounts. This is known as dishonouring (not paying) the note.

### Honouring of Notes Receivable

For example, on July 1, the Alba Company accepts a $9,000 note receivable from Tross Ltd. in settlement of three accounts receivable. The note has an interest rate of 5% per year and is due in six months on December 31.

On December 31, the maturity date, Tross honoured a 6-month note by paying the face or principal amount, $9,000, plus interest of 5%. Assuming that interest has not been accrued, the entry made by Alba is:

| Dec. 31 | Cash | 9,225 | |
|---|---|---|---|
| | Notes Receivable—Tross | | 9,000 |
| | Interest Revenue | | 225 |
| | To record collection of the Tross note | | |

If the interest on the note had been accrued on a monthly basis, then at the end of each month from July through November, the accrual would have been identical to the one illustrated below for July:

| July 31 | Interest Receivable | 37.50 | |
|---|---|---|---|
| | Interest Revenue | | 37.50 |
| | To record interest on the note for the month | | |

At maturity of the note on December 31, the accrued interest would be $187.50 ($37.50 x 5) minus interest from July to November. The interest for December would now be earned. The Alba entry would be as follows:

| Dec. 31 | Cash | 9,225.00 | |
|---|---|---|---|
| | Notes Receivable—Tross | | 9,000.00 |
| | Interest Receivable | | 187.50 |
| | Interest Revenue | | 37.50 |
| | To record collection of the Tross note with accrued interest | | |

### Dishonouring of Notes Receivable

If, on August 31, Tross dishonoured or refused to pay the note, the following entry would be made (assuming interest had not been accrued on a monthly basis):

| Aug. 31 | Accounts Receivable—Tross | 9,225 | |
|---|---|---|---|
| | Notes Receivable | | 9,000 |
| | Interest Revenue | | 225 |

If the amount owing is eventually collected, Alba will debit cash and credit Accounts Receivable. If there were no hope of collection, the principal of the note would be written off by debiting the allowance account and crediting the note receivable account. No interest revenue would be recorded. If the interest were already accrued, the interest amount in the Interest Receivable would be debited.

# Statement Presentation and Management of Receivables

**study objective 4**

Demonstrate the presentation, analysis, and management of receivables.

Financial statement presentation of receivables is important because receivables are directly affected by how a company recognizes its revenue and bad debts expense. The reported numbers are also used when analyzing the liquidity of a company and how well the company manages its receivables.

## Presentation

On the balance sheet, short-term receivables are reported within the current assets section following cash and short-term investments. The net amount of receivables must be disclosed; however, it is helpful to report both the gross amount of receivables and the allowance for doubtful accounts either on the statement or in the notes to the financial statements. Notes receivable are often listed before accounts receivable because they are more easily converted to cash.

## Analysis

The relationship between sales, accounts receivable, and cash collections is important in assessing the company's efficiency. A company's management of its receivables may be helping or hurting it. One way to assess this is to calculate a ratio called the receivables turnover ratio.

The **receivables turnover** ratio measures the number of times, on average, that receivables are collected during a period. The receivables turnover ratio is calculated as follows:

Net Credit Sales ÷ Average Gross Accounts Receivable = Receivables Turnover

A high ratio indicates that the company's receivables are more easily converted into cash. The average gross accounts receivable is calculated using the average of the opening and closing accounts receivable for the period. The receivables turnover is expressed in a figure representing the number of times.

A popular variation of the receivables turnover is to convert it into the number of days it takes the company to collect its receivables. This ratio, called the collection period, is used as a measure of the company's effectiveness in managing its credit sales and converting them to cash. It is calculated as follows:

Days in Year ÷ Receivables Turnover = Collection Period

The collection period is expressed in days. It uses the 365 days in the year divided by the receivables turnover. The higher the receivables turnover, the fewer days it takes to convert the receivables to cash.

The collection period can also be used to assess the length of a company's operating cycle. The combination of the collection period and days to sell inventory is a useful way to measure the length of a company's operating cycle. (See Chapter 6 for the "days to sell inventory".) The calculation is as follows:

Days to Sell Inventory + Collection Period = Operating Cycle in Days

The ratio calculates the number of days, on average, it takes from the time a company purchases its inventory until it collects cash from sales.

## Accelerating Cash Receipts from Receivables

As credit sales and receivables increase in size, waiting for receivables to be collected causes increased costs from not being able to immediately use the cash that will be collected. There are two ways to collect cash more quickly: using the receivables to secure a loan, and selling the receivables.

## Loans Secured by Receivables

To speed up the cash flow, a company can borrow money from the bank using the accounts receivable as collateral. Cash becomes available to the company as the loan is received, and it pays interest on the bank loan. Banks may finance up to 75 percent of the receivables and quite often the arrangement occurs through an operating line of credit.

## Sale of Receivables

Receivables may be sold for cash to another company. Receivables may be sold for the following reasons:

- The company's receivables are very large and the company does not want to hold large amounts of receivables.
- The receivables are the only reasonable source of cash when the company's cash is low and the cost of borrowing may be too high.
- Billing and collection are often too time consuming and costly.

**Factoring** is a way to accelerate receivables collection by selling the receivables to a finance company or bank, known as a factor. The factor will buy the receivables from businesses and then collect the cash directly from the customer.

If the customer does not pay, the business is usually responsible for reimbursing the factor for the uncollected amounts. This is known as selling on a recourse basis.

**Securitization of receivables** is the process of transferring receivables to investors in return for cash. The receivables are sold to an independent trust, which holds the receivables as an investment. This transforms the receivables into securities of the trust. In some cases, the transfer is treated as a sale of receivables or it may be treated as a secured loan.

# Demonstration Problem (SO 1, 2, & 3)

The December 31, 2007, balance sheet of Sparkle City Company reported the following amounts:

| | |
|---|---|
| Accounts Receivable | $180,000 |
| Allowance for Doubtful Accounts | 4,200 |

The following transactions occurred during the year:

| | | |
|---|---|---|
| Jan. | 1 | Accepted Barber Consultants' $10,000, 9-month, 12% note for the balance due on account. Interest is accrued every three months. |
| Feb. | 5 | Wrote off as uncollectible an account receivable from Stoldt Co. for $750 and an account receivable from Scanlon for $1,200. |
| Mar. | 31 | Interest on the note accepted from Barber Consultants was accrued to date. |
| May | 26 | Received $1,200 from Scanlon for the account receivable written off on February 5. |
| June | 30 | Interest on the note accepted from Barber Consultants was accrued from April 1 to date. |
| July | 15 | Received a 2-month, 6% note from Hammond to replace her account receivable balance of $5,000. |
| Sep. | 15 | Hammond dishonoured her note. It is expected that Hammond will still pay in the future. |

Oct.        31      Barber Consultants honours its Note Receivable, and has sent the
                    company a cheque in the amount owing plus interest to date.

Dec.        15      Hammond declared bankruptcy. Her account is written off as
                    uncollectible.

Dec.        31      Using the percentage of sales approach, Sparkle City estimates that 2% of
                    credit sales will become uncollectible. Credit sales for the year are
                    $500,000.

## Instructions

(a)  Prepare the journal entries for Sparkle City's transactions.
(b)  Calculate the balance in the Allowance for Doubtful Accounts on December 31, 2008.

## Solution to Demonstration Problem

| General Journal | | | J1 |
|---|---|---|---|
| **Date** | **Account Titles and Explanation** | **Debit** | **Credit** |
| 2008 | | | |
| (a) | | | |
| Jan.   31 | Notes Receivable—Barber | 10,000 | |
| | Accounts Receivable—Barber | | 10,000 |
| | To record acceptance of Barber | | |
| | Consultants note. | | |
| | | | |
| Feb.   5 | Allowance for Doubtful Accounts | 750 | |
| | Accounts Receivable—Stoldt | | 750 |
| | To write off account of Stoldt's accounts | | |
| | receivable. | | |
| | | | |
| | Allowance for Doubtful Accounts | 1,200 | |
| | Accounts Receivable—Scanlon | | 1,200 |
| | To write off account of Scanlon. | | |
| | | | |
| Mar.   31 | Interest Receivable—Barber | 300 | |
| | Interest Revenue | | 300 |
| | To record interest accrued from January 1 | | |
| | to date ($10,000 x 12% x 3/12) | | |

| Date | Account Titles and Explanation | Debit | Credit |
|---|---|---|---|
| May 26 | Accounts Receivable—Scanlon | 1,200 | |
| |     Allowance for Doubtful Accounts | | 1,200 |
| | To reverse the Scanlon write off entry. | | |
| | | | |
| | Cash | 1,200 | |
| |     Accounts Receivable—Scanlon | | 1,200 |
| | To record collection from Scanlon. | | |
| | | | |
| June 30 | Interest Receivable | 300 | |
| |     Interest Revenue | | 300 |
| | To record interest from April 1 to date. | | |
| | | | |
| July 15 | Notes Receivable | 5,000 | |
| |     Accounts Receivable | | 5,000 |
| | To receive a note to replace an account. | | |
| | | | |
| Sept. 15 | Accounts Receivable | 5,050 | |
| |     Interest Revenue ($5,000 × 6% × 2/12) | | 50 |
| |     Notes Receivable | | 5,000 |
| | To record Hammond's dishonoured note. | | |
| | | | |
| Oct. 31 | Cash | 10,900 | |
| |     Interest Revenue | | 300 |
| |     Interest Receivable | | 600 |
| |     Notes Receivable | | 10,000 |
| | To record Barber's note honoured. | | |
| | | | |
| Dec. 15 | Allowance for Doubtful Accounts | 5,050 | |
| |     Accounts Receivable | | 5,050 |
| | To record write off of Hammond's account. | | |
| | | | |
| 31 | Bad Debts Expense ($500,000 × 2%) | 10,000 | |
| |     Allowance for Doubtful Accounts | | 10,000 |
| | To record estimated bad debts. | | |

(b)

| | | | |
|---|---|---|---|
| Balance, Jan. 1, 2008 | Allowance for Doubtful Accounts | | $4,200 Cr. |
| Receivable write off | Stoldt | $ 750 | |
| Receivable write off | Scanlon | 1,200 | |
| Receivable reversal | Scanlon | (1,200) | |
| Receivable write off | Hammond | 5,050 | 5,800 Dr. |
| Balance before allowance set up | | | 1,600 Dr. |
| | | | |
| December 31 estimate of uncollectible accounts | | | 10,000 Cr. |
| Balance, Dec. 31, 2008 | | | $8,400 Cr. |

# Review Questions and Exercises

## Multiple Choice

Circle the letter that best answers each of the following statements.

1. (SO 1) Which of the following are also called trade receivables?

    a. Accounts receivable
    b. Other receivables
    c. Advances to employees
    d. Recoverable income taxes

2. (SO 1) On February 1, 2008, Lara Company sells merchandise on account to Livingston Company for $5,000. Lara Company uses the periodic inventory system. The entry to record this transaction by Lara Company is:

    a. Sales                         5,000
        Accounts Payable                     5,000
    b. Cash                          5,000
        Sales                                5,000
    c. Accounts Receivable           5,000
        Sales                                5,000
    d. Notes Receivable              5,000
        Accounts Receivable                  5,000

3. (SO 1) On March 1, 2008, Etheredge Company sells merchandise on account to Brooks Company for $7,000, terms n/30. Etheredge Company uses the periodic inventory system. On March 8, payment is received from Brooks for the balance due. The entry on March 8 by Etheredge is:

    a. Sales                         7,000
        Accounts Payable                     7,000
    b. Cash                          7,000
        Sales                                7,000
    c. Cash                          7,000
        Accounts Receivable                  7,000
    d. Notes Receivable              7,000
        Accounts Receivable                  7,000

4. (SO 1) When an Accounts Receivable is recognized it is posted to the general ledger, which acts as a control account, and also to:

   a. the sales account, where the individual amount owing is recognized.
   b. the subsidiary ledger, where the individual accounts receivable is recognized.
   c. the merchandise inventory, as a debit to recognize the goods sold.
   d. the sales account, to recognize the cost of the items sold.

5. (SO 1) When interest is charged to a customer's account, all the following occur except:

   a. the customer's subsidiary accounts receivable increases.
   b. the seller recognizes an accrual of revenue.
   c. the account Interest Receivable is increased.
   d. the resulting effect is an increase in net income.

6. (SO 2) When the allowance method of recognizing bad debts expense is used, the entry to recognize that expense:

   a. increases net income.
   b. decreases current assets.
   c. has no effect on current assets.
   d. has no effect on net income.

7. (SO 2) An approach of estimating uncollectible accounts that focuses on the income statement rather than the balance sheet is the:

   a. direct write off of uncollectibles.
   b. aging of the accounts receivable.
   c. percentage of sales.
   d. percentage of receivables.

8. (SO 2) White Company estimates bad debts expense at 2% of credit sales. The following data are available for 2008:

   | | |
   |---|---|
   | Allowance for doubtful accounts, 1/1/08 | $ 21,000 (Cr.) |
   | Accounts written off as uncollectible during 2008 | 13,000 |
   | Credit sales in 2008 | 3,000,000 |

   The Allowance for Doubtful Accounts balance at December 31, 2008, should be:

   a. $68,000.
   b. $60,000.
   c. $50,000.
   d. $13,000.

9. (SO 2) In 2008, the Rabindra Company had credit sales of $600,000 and granted sales allowances of $12,000. On January 1, 2008, Allowance for Doubtful Accounts had a credit balance of $15,000. During 2008, $25,000 of uncollectible accounts receivable were written off. Experience indicates that 3% of net credit sales become uncollectible. What should be the adjusted balance of Allowance for Doubtful Accounts at December 31, 2008?

   a. $7,640
   b. $8,000
   c. $17,640
   d. $33,000

10. (SO 2) An analysis and aging of the accounts receivable of Green Company at December 31 revealed the following data:

Accounts Receivable                                 $600,000

Allowance for Doubtful Accounts

   before adjustment                          75,000 (Cr.)

Estimated uncollectible accounts          82,000

The net realizable value of the accounts receivable at December 31, after adjustment, is:

a. $583,000.

b. $525,000.

c. $518,000.

d. $443,000.

11. (SO 2) Voight Company's account balances at December 31 for Accounts Receivable and Allowance for Doubtful Accounts were $1,400,000 and $70,000 (Cr.), respectively. An aging of accounts receivable indicated that $108,000 is expected to become uncollectible. The amount of the adjusting entry for bad debts at December 31 is:

a. $108,000.

b. $38,000.

c. $178,000.

d. $70,000.

12. (SO 2) Bonnie Company decides that the past due account of Sheldon Stahl is uncollectible. Under the allowance method, the $865 balance owed by Sheldon Stahl is written off as follows:

a. Bad Debts Expense                       865

       Accounts Receivable—S. Stahl             865

b. Allowance for Doubtful Accounts       865

       Accounts Receivable—S. Stahl             865

c. Accounts Receivable—S. Stahl         865

       Allowance for Doubtful Accounts         865

d. Allowance for Doubtful Accounts       865

       Bad Debts Expense                      865

13. (SO 2) On October 18, the Aurora Company realizes that the $300 balance of Mary Vonesh that was written off as uncollectible is now collectible. The entry to restore the customer's account is:

a. Allowance for Doubtful Accounts       300

       Accounts Receivable—Mary Vonesh     300

b. Bad Debts Expense                       300

       Allowance for Doubtful Accounts         300

c. Accounts Receivable—Mary Vonesh     300

       Allowance for Doubtful Accounts         300

d. Accounts Receivable—Mary Vonesh     300

       Bad Debts Expense                      300

14. (SO 3) On February 1, Lowery Company received a $5,000, 9%, 4-month note receivable. Interest is due at maturity. The cash to be received by Lowery Company when the note becomes due is:

   a.  $150.
   b.  $5,000.
   c.  $5,150.
   d.  $5,450.

Questions 15 and 16 are based on the following information: On February 15, 2008, Gilbert Company received a 3-month, 9%, $2,000 note from Vincent Nathan for the settlement of his account receivable.

15. (SO 3) The entry by Gilbert Company on February 15, 2008 is:

   a.  Notes Receivable                           2,000
          Accounts Receivable—V. Nathan                    2,000
   b.  Accounts Receivable—V. Nathan            2,045
          Notes Receivable                                 2,045
   c.  Cash                                      2,045
          Interest Revenue                                    45
          Notes Receivable                                 2,000
   d.  Cash                                      2,000
          Accounts Receivable—V. Nathan                    2,000

16. (SO 3) The entry by Gilbert Company on May 15, 2008, if Nathan dishonours the note and collection as expected is:

   a.  Accounts Receivable—V. Nathan            2,045
          Notes Receivable                                 2,045
   b.  Accounts Receivable—V. Nathan            2,045
          Notes Receivable                                 2,000
          Interest Revenue                                    45
   c.  Accounts Receivable—V. Nathan            1,855
       Interest Lost                               45
          Notes Receivable                                 2,000
   d.  Bad Debts Expense                         2,045
          Notes Receivable                                 2,045

17. (SO 3) All of the following are true except:

   a.  An account receivable is an informal promise to pay an amount owing.
   b.  An account receivable is the same as a note receivable.
   c.  A note receivable is a written promise to pay an amount owing.
   d.  A note receivable can be transferred to another party by endorsement.

18. (SO 3) A note receivable could have which of the following characteristics:

    a.  It bears interest for the period of the note.
    b.  It could result from a purchase or a loan.
    c.  It could result from extending an account receivable beyond normal amounts or due dates.
    d.  It could be a result of all or any of the above.

19. (SO 3) Which on of the following statements about notes receivable and accounts receivable is correct?

    a.  They are both interest bearing for the period that they exist.
    b.  They are both credit instruments.
    c.  They are both valued at their net realizable values.
    d.  They can be sold to another party.

20. (SO 4) In the financial statement presentation of receivables:

    a.  it is not necessary to identify the major types of receivables.
    b.  both the gross amount of receivables and the allowance for doubtful accounts must be disclosed.
    c.  bad debts are reported as an operating expense on the income statement.
    d.  accounts receivable are always listed before notes receivable because accounts receivable are more important.

21. (SO 4) A company may sell its receivables for any of the following reasons except:

    a.  it needs cash and may not be able to borrow money in the credit market.
    b.  it does not want to hold a large amount of receivables.
    c.  the billing and collection of receivables are costly and time consuming.
    d.  the billing and collection is not acceptable and it is converting to a cash-only system.

22. (SO 3, 4) Which of the following statements concerning receivables is incorrect?

    a.  Notes receivable are often listed last under receivables.
    b.  Notes receivable give the maker a stronger legal claim to assets than accounts receivable.
    c.  Both the gross amount of receivables and the allowance for doubtful accounts should be reported.
    d.  Interest revenue and gain on sale of notes receivable are shown under other revenues and gains.

## Matching

Match each term with its definition by writing the appropriate letter in the space provided.

**Terms**

_____ 1. Promissory note

_____ 2. Aging of accounts receivable

_____ 3. Percentage of sales approach

_____ 4. Allowance method

_____ 5. Percentage of receivables approach

_____ 6. Net realizable value

_____ 7. Dishonoured note

_____ 8. Honoured note

_____ 9. Maker

_____ 10. Payee

**Definitions**

a. An approach to estimating uncollectible accounts where bad debts expense is calculated as a percentage of credit sales.

b. The net amount of receivables expected to be received in cash.

c. A method of accounting for bad debts that is required when bad debts are material.

d. The party that promises to pay a promissory note.

e. A note that is not paid in full at maturity.

f. A written promise to pay a specified amount of money on demand or at a definite time.

g. An approach to estimating uncollectible accounts where the allowance for doubtful accounts is calculated as a percentage of receivables.

h. An analysis of individual customer accounts by the length of time they have been unpaid.

i. The party to whom a promissory note is to be paid.

j. A note that is paid in full at maturity.

# Exercises

**E8-1** (SO 2) The L. Riel Co. had a credit balance in Allowance for Doubtful Accounts of $10,000 at January 1, 2008. During 2008, credit sales totalled $300,000. A summary of the aging of accounts receivable at December 31, 2008 is as follows:

| Classification by Month of Sale | Balance in Each Category | Estimated % Uncollectible |
|---|---|---|
| Nov. – Dec., 2008 | $ 60,000 | 2% |
| Jul. – Oct., 2008 | 30,000 | 10 |
| Jan. – June, 2008 | 10,000 | 25 |
| Prior to 1/1/08 | 5,000 | 75 |
| | $105,000 | |

On April 2, 2008, $750 was received from Tom Scott; his account for $750 had been written off as uncollectible in 2004. During 2008, accounts receivable totalling $8,400 were written off as uncollectible.

## Instructions

(a) Record the April 2 collection of the account previously written off.

(b) Prepare a summary entry for the accounts written off in 2008 dated Dec. 31.

(c) Assuming L. Riel Co. estimates uncollectibles as 2% of credit sales, prepare the December 31, 2008, adjusting entry.

(d) Instead assume that L. Riel Co. estimates uncollectibles by using the percentage of accounts receivable. Prepare the December 31, 2008, adjusting entry (use the aging schedule if necessary).

| General Journal | | | J1 |
|---|---|---|---|
| **Date** | **Account Titles and Explanation** | **Debit** | **Credit** |
| 2008 | | | |
| (a) | | | |
| | | | |
| | | | |
| | | | |
| | | | |
| | | | |
| | | | |
| | | | |
| (b) | | | |
| | | | |
| | | | |
| | | | |
| | | | |
| (c) | | | |
| | | | |
| | | | |
| | | | |
| | | | |
| | | | |
| (d) | | | |
| | | | |
| | | | |
| | | | |
| | | | |
| | | | |
| | | | |

**E8-2**   (SO 3) Burton Company had the following transactions for the year ended December 31, 2008:

July  1  Received a $2,000, 3-month, 8% promissory note from Richard Newman in settlement of an open account. Interest is payable at maturity.

Aug.  1  Received a $1,000, 3-month, 10% note receivable from Suzanne Hurley for cash borrowed by Hurley. Interest is payable at maturity.

Oct.  1  Received notice that the Richard Newman note had been dishonoured. It is expected that Newman will eventually pay the amount owed.

Nov.  1  Hurley honoured the note receivable in full. (Assume that interest has not been accrued.)

### Instructions
Prepare the entries for the transactions above.

| General Journal | | | JI |
|---|---|---|---|
| **Date** | **Account Titles and Explanation** | **Debit** | **Credit** |
| 2008 | | | |
| | | | |
| | | | |
| | | | |
| | | | |
| | | | |
| | | | |
| | | | |
| | | | |
| | | | |
| | | | |
| | | | |
| | | | |
| | | | |
| | | | |
| | | | |
| | | | |
| | | | |
| | | | |

**E8-3**    (SO 3) The Bego Company adjusts its books monthly. On June 30, 2008, selected ledger account balances are as follows:

|  |  |
|---|---|
| Notes Receivable | $44,200 |
| Interest Receivable | 315 |

Notes Receivable include the following:

| Date | Maker | Principal | Interest | Term |
|---|---|---|---|---|
| Apr. 1 | Karam Inc. | $10,000 | 7% | 6 months |
| May 1 | Lyttle Co. | 9,000 | 5% | 3 months |
| June 1 | Meyer Inc. | 6,000 | 10% | 6 months |
| June 15 | Sulit Ltd. | 7,200 | 5% | 4 months |
| June 30 | Rinas Corp. | 12,000 | 9% | 6 months |

## Instructions

(a) Prepare a schedule calculating the Interest Receivable at June 30.

(b) Prepare the entry to record the full payment of the Karam note at maturity on September 30, 2008 (round answers to the nearest dollar).

(a) _____

_____

_____

_____

_____

_____

(b) _____

_____

_____

_____

_____

_____

_____

**E8-4**    (SO 1 & 3)

(a)    On May 1, 2009, the Shaloy Company sold merchandise to E. Dale. She used her Shaloy credit card, which has an interest charge of 20% per annum. On the payment date on her statement, June 3, she was not able to pay the balance of her account, $3,000, and was charged a financing charge for the first month she was overdue.

(b)    Everson Retailers, a customer of the Shaloy Company, had signed a promissory note that was due on June 1. The note, in the amount of $10,000 at 6% for three months, was accepted when three invoices from Everson remained unpaid. Interest is to be accrued monthly.

## Instructions

(a) Record Shaloy's entry on June 3 to record the interest charged to E. Dale.

(b) Record Shaloy's entry to record accepting the note receivable from Everson.

(c) Record the interest accrued on the Everson note at the end of the first month.

(d) Why is the interest on the overdue accounts receivable added to the customer account, but the interest on the note receivable is recorded separately?

(a)

(b)

(c)

(d)

**E8-5**     (SO 4) The following information was taken from the records of the Minimoore Company:

| | |
|---|---|
| Accounts Receivable December 31, 2008 | $235,000 |
| Accounts Receivable December 31, 2007 | $189,000 |
| Sales | $1,535,000 |
| Sales Returns and Allowances | $35,000 |
| Allowance for Doubtful Accounts 2007 | $28,000 |
| Allowance for Doubtful Accounts 2008 | $30,000 |

## Instructions

(a) Calculate (1) the receivables turnover and (2) the collection period.

(b) If the receivables turnover for the previous year was 20 times and the collection period was 18.25 days, comment on the company's performance over the two years.

# Solutions to Review Questions and Exercises

## Multiple Choice

1.  (a)   Accounts receivable, also called trade receivables, are amounts owed by customers on account. Answer (b), other receivables, include non-trade receivables. Advances to employees (c) and recoverable income taxes (d) are included under the category of other receivables.

2.  (c)   When a business sells merchandise on credit, in addition to the revenue earned and recorded as Sales, it must recognize the increase to Accounts Receivable by debiting the asset account.

3.  (c)   The correct entry is Cash (Dr.) $7,000 and Accounts Receivable (Cr.) $7,000.

4.  (b)   Receivables are posted to the Accounts Receivable—a control account—and also to the Subsidiary Accounts Receivable ledger, where individual customer accounts are kept.

5.  (c)   Items (a), (b), and (d) are all true. The exception is item (c), where interest is not debited to Interest Receivable. It is debited to the Accounts Receivable account and to the customer's subsidiary account to recognize the additional interest amount owing.

6.  (b)   Estimated uncollectibles are debited to Bad Debts Expense and credited to Allowance for Doubtful Accounts. The Allowance for Doubtful Accounts is a contra asset account to Accounts Receivable. When it is offset against Accounts Receivable, it decreases the current assets to its net realizable value.

7.  (c)   The allowance method using the percentage of sales approach focuses on the income statement. The aging of the accounts receivable (b) and a percentage of the accounts receivable (d) focus on the balance sheet.

8.  (a)   The balance in the Allowance for Doubtful Accounts prior to adjustment is a credit of $8,000 ($21,000 – $13,000). The adjusting entry under the percentage of sales method is $60,000 ($3,000,000 x 2%). Thus, the adjusted balance is $68,000 ($8,000 + $60,000).

9.  (a)   The balance in Allowance for Doubtful Accounts prior to adjustment is a debit of $10,000 ($25,000 – $15,000). The adjusting entry is $17,640 [($600,000 – $12,000) x 3%]. Thus the ending balance is $7,640 ($17,640 – $10,000).

10. (c)   The net realizable value of the accounts receivable at December 31 should be accounts receivable ($600,000) less the ending balance of the allowance for doubtful accounts ($82,000), or $518,000.

11. (b)   Under the percentage of receivables approach, the allowance account is adjusted to the estimated uncollectibles. In this case, the required balance is $108,000 and the amount of the adjusting entry is $38,000 ($108,000 – $70,000).

12.  (b)  Under the allowance method, every bad debt write off is made against the allowance account. The write off of the account reduces both Accounts Receivable and Allowance for Doubtful Accounts. A debit to Bad Debts Expense is used only when the adjusting entry is made for estimated bad debts.

13.  (c)  When an uncollectible account already written off becomes collectible, the entry to restore the customer account is a debit to Accounts Receivable and a credit to the Allowance for Doubtful Accounts.

14.  (c)  When a Note Receivable becomes due, interest together with the principal amount is due to the maker of the note. Interest calculated ($5,000 x 9% x 4/12 = $150) is added to the principal of $5,000. Total cash received is $5,150.

15.  (a)  A transfer from one asset account, Accounts Receivable, to another asset account, Notes Receivable, is made by debiting Notes Receivable and crediting Accounts Receivable.

16.  (b)  If the note is dishonoured, the Notes Receivable reverts to Accounts Receivable. The amount of interest that has been earned, $45 ($2,000 x 9% x 3/12), is recognized by crediting interest revenue and by increasing Accounts Receivable.

17.  (b)  An account receivable is different from a note receivable. A note gives the payee a stronger legal claim to the amount owing.

18.  (d)  Items (a), (b), and (c) are all characteristics of notes receivable.

19.  (a)  Accounts receivable do not incur interest unless the account is overdue. Notes receivable usually bear interest for the entire period.

20.  (c)  Bad debts expense is included in operating expenses because bad debts are the result of an operating decision—the decision to sell on credit.

21.  (d)  Most companies extend credit to attract customers. Changing to a cash-only system is not good for business nor is it a reason to sell the receivables. Items (a), (b), and (c) are the reasons receivables are sold.

22.  (a)  Notes receivable are often listed before accounts receivables because the notes give the maker a stronger legal claim to assets than accounts receivable.  Answers (b), (c) and (d) are all correct.

## Matching

| | | | | | |
|---|---|---|---|---|---|
| 1. | f | 5. | g | 9. | d |
| 2. | h | 6. | b | 10. | i |
| 3. | a | 7. | e | | |
| 4. | c | 8. | j | | |

# Exercises

E8-1

| General Journal | | | JI |
|---|---|---|---|
| **Date** | **Account Titles and Explanation** | **Debit** | **Credit** |
| 2008 | | | |
| (a) | | | |
| April    2 | Accounts Receivable—T. Scott | 750 | |
| | Allowance for Doubtful Accounts | | 750 |
| | To reverse write off of T. Scott account. | | |
| | | | |
| 2 | Cash | 750 | |
| | Accounts Receivable—T. Scott | | 750 |
| | To record collection from T. Scott. | | |
| (b) | | | |
| Dec.    31 | Allowance for Doubtful Accounts | 8,400 | |
| | Accounts Receivable | | 8,400 |
| | To write off 2008 uncollectible accounts. | | |
| | | | |
| (c) | | | |
| Dec.    31 | Bad Debts Expense ($300,000 x 2%) | 6,000 | |
| | Allowance for Doubtful Accounts | | 6,000 |
| | To record estimated bad debts for year. | | |
| | | | |
| (d) | | | |
| Dec.    31 | Bad Debts Expense | 8,100 | |
| | Allowance for Doubtful Accounts | | 8,100* |
| | To adjust allowance account to total estimated uncollectibles. | | |

* The balance in Allowance for Doubtful Accounts prior to adjustment is $2,350 (Cr.) ($10,000 + $750 - $8,400). Therefore, the adjusting entry is $8,100 ($10,450 - $2,350).

(d) cont.

## Aging Schedule

| Classification by Month of Sale | Balance in Each Category | Estimated % Uncollectible | Estimated Bad Debts |
|---|---|---|---|
| Nov. — Dec. 2008 | $ 60,000 | 2% | $ 1,200 |
| July — Oct. 2008 | 30,000 | 10 | 3,000 |
| Jan. — June 2008 | 10,000 | 25 | 2,500 |
| Prior to 1/1/03 | 5,000 | 75 | 3,750 |
| | $105,000 | | $10,450 |

### E8-2

| General Journal | | | JI |
|---|---|---|---|
| **Date** | **Account Titles and Explanation** | **Debit** | **Credit** |
| 2008 | | | |
| July    1 | Notes Receivable | 2,000 | |
| | Accounts Receivable—R. Newman | | 2,000 |
| | To record acceptance of R. Newman note. | | |
| | | | |
| Aug.    1 | Note Receivable | 1,000 | |
| | Cash | | 1,000 |
| | To record acceptance of S. Hurley note. | | |
| | | | |
| Oct.    1 | Accounts Receivable | 2,040 | |
| | Notes Receivable | | 2,000 |
| | Interest Revenue ($2,000 x 8% x 3/12) | | 40 |
| | To record dishonouring of the R. Newman | | |
| | note; expect to collect in the future. | | |
| | | | |
| Nov.    1 | Cash | 1,025 | |
| | Notes Receivable | | 1,000 |
| | Interest Revenue ($1,000 x 10% x 3/12) | | 25 |
| | To record honouring of S. Hurley note. | | |

**E8-3**

(a)

| | | | |
|---|---|---|---|
| Karam Inc. | $10,000 x 7% x 3/12 | = | $175.00 |
| Lyttle Co. | $ 9,000 x 5% x 2/12 | = | 75.00 |
| Meyer Inc. | $ 6,000 x 10% x 1/12 | = | 50.00 |
| Sulit Ltd. | $ 7,200 x 5% x 0.5/12 | = | 15.00 |
| | | | $315.00 |

(b)
2008

| | | | |
|---|---|---|---|
| Sept. 30 | Cash | 10,350 | |
| | Notes Receivable | | 10,000 |
| | Interest Receivable (5 months accrued) | | 292 |
| | Interest Revenue | | 58 |
| | To record payment of note at maturity | | |

**E8-4**

| | | | | |
|---|---|---|---|---|
| (a) | June 3 | Accounts Receivable—Dale | 50 | |
| | | Interest Revenue | | 50 |
| | | To record service fees on overdue account | | |

| | | | | |
|---|---|---|---|---|
| (b) | June 1 | Note Receivable | 10,000 | |
| | | Accounts Receivable | | 10,000 |
| | | To record acceptance of Everson's note | | |

| | | | | |
|---|---|---|---|---|
| (c) | June 30 | Interest Receivable | 50 | |
| | | Interest Revenue | | 50 |
| | | To record interest accrued on note | | |

(d) Though both accounts receivable and notes receivable are interest bearing, interest charges are added to the balance due if a customer does not pay the account in full within a specified period (usually 30 days). The interest on the notes payable becomes due at the maturity of the notes payable as the legal claim states and is not due until the note's maturity date. Also, the note receivable remains at its historical cost.

**E8-5**

(a) (1) Receivables turnover = $1,500,000 ÷ ([235,000 + 189,000] ÷ 2)

= $1,500,000 ÷ $212,000

= 7 times

(2) Collection period = 365 ÷ 7

= 52 days

(b) The receivables turnover measures the company's efficiency in converting its credit sales into cash. The collection period is used to assess the effectiveness of the credit and collection policy. The receivables turnover has dropped from 20 times to 7 times. That means that the company efficiency in converting credit sales to cash has decreased. The collection period has increased from 18.25 days to 52 days. The company has not collected as efficiently in this period and should reconsider its credit and collection policies.

chapter 9
# Long-Lived Assets

## study objectives >>

After studying this chapter, you should be able to:
1. Apply the cost principle to property, plant, and equipment.
2. Explain and calculate amortization.
3. Revise periodic amortization.
4. Account for the disposal of property, plant, and equipment.
5. Calculate and record amortization of natural resources.
6. Identify the basic accounting issues for intangible assets.
7. Illustrate the reporting and analysis of long-lived assets.

# Preview of Chapter 9

In this chapter, we explain the application of the cost principle of accounting to long-lived assets such as property, plant, and equipment; natural resources; and intangible assets. We also describe the methods used to allocate an asset's cost over its useful life. In addition, we discuss the accounting for expenditures incurred during the useful life of assets and the disposition of the assets at the end of their useful lives. The chapter is organized as follows:

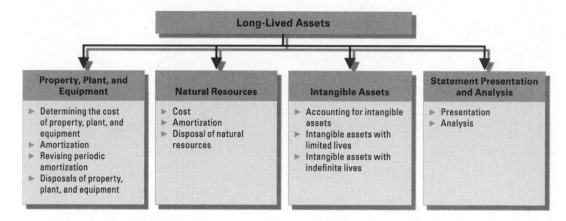

# Property, Plant, and Equipment

**Property, plant, and equipment** are long-lived assets that are used for the production and sale of goods and/or services to consumers. They are often subdivided into four classes:
1. Land, such as a building site
2. Land improvements, such as fences and parking lots, which are not permanent fixtures
3. Buildings, such as stores, offices, and factories
4. Equipment, such as cash registers, machinery, and office furniture

## Determining the Cost of Property, Plant, and Equipment

study objective 1

Apply the cost principle to property, plant, and equipment.

Property, plant, and equipment are recorded at cost. Cost includes all expenditures made to acquire the asset and make it ready for its intended use. For example, if you buy land with an old building on it and you intend to erect a new building, the cost of wrecking the old building becomes a cost of the land. The wrecking costs are capitalized, not expensed.

Costs that benefit only the current period are expensed. Costs that are capitalized rather than expensed will provide benefits over future periods. These costs are called capital expenditures. Once the cost of an asset is established, it becomes the basis of accounting for the asset over its useful life.

Even if or when an asset increases in value, the current market value is not used after the asset is acquired. Cost is only adjusted if there is a permanent decline of the asset below the book value.

### Land
The cost of land includes the purchase price, closing costs such as surveying and legal fees, and the costs of preparing the land for its intended use. All these costs become part of the total cost of the land and would be debited to the Land account, with the credit going to whichever account closely explains the means of purchase, such as Cash or Mortgage Payable. Land is the only asset whose service potential does not decline over its useful life, so it is not amortized.

### Land Improvements

Land improvements are structural additions made to the land. Land improvements such as driveways, parking lots, and landscaping require maintenance and replacement to retain their value. They have limited useful lives and are amortized over their useful lives. These costs are recorded separately from the cost of land.

### Buildings

The costs debited to the Buildings accounts include all costs related to the purchase or construction of a building. Costs include the purchase price, closing costs (such as legal fees), and costs to make the building ready for its intended use, such as remodelling and replacing or repairing the roof, floors, wiring, and plumbing.

When a new building is constructed, costs consist of the contract price plus payments made for architects' fees, building permits, and excavation costs. Interest payments on funds borrowed for the construction are included in the asset cost when there is a considerable amount of time needed to get the building ready for use. Once the building is ready for use, further interest payments are debited to Interest Expenses.

### Equipment

Equipment includes delivery equipment, office equipment, machinery, vehicles, furniture and fixtures, and other similar assets. The cost of equipment consists of the purchase price and other related costs, such as freight charges and insurance during transit, paid by the purchaser. Other included costs are all expenditures required to assemble, install, and test the unit. These costs are capitalized.

All capitalized costs benefit future periods. Annual recurring costs such as licences and insurance are not capitalized because they do not benefit future periods.

### Basket Purchase

The purchase of property, plant, and equipment, often purchased as a group for a single price, is known as a **basket purchase**. The total price paid for the group of property, plant, and equipment must be allocated to each individual asset. Total cost should be allocated to each individual asset based on its relative **fair market value**.

## Amortization

**Amortization** is the allocation of the cost of a long-lived asset to expense over its useful (service) life. The cost allocation matches expenses with revenues in accordance with the matching principle. It is done in a rational and systematic way.

study objective 2

Explain and calculate amortization.

Amortization is a cost allocation. It is not the accumulation of cash for the replacement of the asset. Rather it is the allocation of the cost of using up the asset over its useful life. As the asset's useful years increase, its revenue-producing ability decreases because of physical wear and tear.

When the adjustment for amortization is recorded, the entry debits Amortization Expense and credits Accumulated Amortization. The accumulated amortization account is a contra account to its related amortizable asset account. Thus, the asset account (DR), less its contra account, Accumulated Amortization (CR), gives the asset's net book value.

Land improvements, buildings, and equipment are amortizable assets because their usefulness to the company and their revenue-producing ability decrease during their useful lives. Land is not amortized because its life is unlimited and its ability to produce revenue is generally the same over time.

Amortization is only an estimate of the asset's decline in value. Sometimes a decline in an asset's revenue-producing ability may occur because of obsolescence. For example, a company may replace its computers long before they wear out because of hardware and software improvements.

### Factors in Calculating Amortization
Three factors affect the calculation of amortization:
1. **Cost** includes all costs incurred to obtain the asset and make it ready for its intended use.
2. **Useful life** is an estimate of the asset's expected productive life or service life.
3. **Residual value** is an estimate of the asset's value at the end of its useful life.

### Amortization Methods
Amortization is generally calculated using one of three methods:
1. Straight-line
2. Declining-balance
3. Units-of-activity

Each method is acceptable under generally accepted accounting principles. Management selects the method that it believes will best measure the asset's contribution to revenue during its useful life. Once the method is chosen, it should be consistently applied. Consistency makes financial statement comparisons easier.

**Straight-Line.** Under the straight-line method, amortization is the same for each year of the asset's useful life.

The formula for calculating annual amortization expense is:

Cost − Residual Value = Amortizable Cost

Amortizable Cost ÷ Estimated Useful Life = Amortization Expense

For example, assume that the Benson Company purchased a delivery truck for $31,000 on January 1, with an estimated residual value of $1,000 at the end of its four-year service life. The calculation of annual amortization would be as follows:

($31,000 − $1,000) ÷ 4 =    $7,500

Alternatively, straight-line amortization can be calculated by dividing 100% by the estimated useful life of the asset and applying that rate to the amortizable cost.
Using the example above:

(100% ÷ 4 years) x ($31,000 - $1,000) = amortization expense

25%    x    $30,000    =    $7,500

When the asset is purchased during the year, amortization expense is pro-rated for the time the asset was used. Calculation should be rounded to the nearest month since amortization is an estimate.

The straight-line method is commonly used and simple to apply. It matches expenses and revenues appropriately when the use of the asset is reasonably uniform throughout its useful life, as in the case of a building.

**Declining-Balance.** The declining-balance method produces a decreasing annual amortization expense over the asset's useful life. Unlike other amortization methods, the declining-balance method does not use amortizable cost. The residual value limits the total amortization that can be taken. Amortization stops when the asset's book value equals its expected residual value.

The formula for calculating amortization expense using the declining-balance method is:
Net Book Value at Beginning of Year x Declining-Balance Rate = Amortization Expense

For example, the Benson Company uses a declining-balance rate of 40% to amortize an asset that cost $31,000. The estimated residual value is $1,000. Amortization is calculated as follows:

| Year | Net Book Value Beginning of Year | | Amortization Rate | | Amortization Expense | Net Book Value End of Year |
|------|----------------------------------|---|-------------------|---|----------------------|----------------------------|
| 1 | $31,000 | − | 40% | = | $12,400 | $(31,000 - 12,400) |
| 2 | $18,600 | − | 40% | = | $ 7,440 | $(31,000 - 19,840) |
| 3 | $11,160 | − | 40% | = | $ 4,464 | $(31,000 - 24,304) |
| 4 | $ 6,696 | − | 40% | = | $ 5,696* | $(31,000 - 30,000) |

*the amortization expense for year 4, calculated using the amortization rate, is $2,678 (rounded to the nearest dollar). However, this is the end of the asset's useful life so amortization is calculated so that net book value equals its estimated residual value. The residual value is accounted for at the end of the amortization process, rather than at the beginning.

Under the declining-balance method, the amortization rate remains constant from year to year, but the net book value to which the rate is applied declines each year. The declining-balance method is considered an **accelerated amortization method**.

The declining-balance method is compatible with the matching principle because the higher amortization in early years is matched with the higher benefits received in these years. When an asset is purchased during the year, the first year's amortization must be pro-rated for the time the asset was used.

Varying rates of amortization may be used, depending on how fast the company wants to amortize the asset. You will find rates such as one time (single), two times (double), and even three times (triple) the straight-line rate of amortization. An amortization rate that is often used is double the straight-line rate. This method is referred to as the double declining-balance method.

**Units-of-Activity.** Under the units-of-activity method, useful life is expressed in terms of the total units of production or activity expected from the asset.

For example, the Benson Company has a truck purchased for $31,000 and expects to drive the truck for 200,000 kilometres. The estimated residual value is $1,000. In the first year the truck is driven 30,000 kilometres. The formula for calculating amortization expense is:

| | | | | | |
|---|---|---|---|---|---|
| 1. | Cost | − | Residual Value | = | Amortizable Cost |
| | $31,000 | − | $1,000 | = | $30,000 |
| | | | | | |
| 2. | Amortizable Cost | ÷ | Total Estimated Units of Activity | = | Amortizable Cost per Unit |
| | $30,000 | ÷ | 200,000 km | = | $0.15 |
| | | | | | |
| 3. | Amortization Cost per Unit | − | Units of Activity During the Year | = | Annual Amortization Expense |
| | $0.15 | x | 30,000 km | = | $4,500 |

In using this units-of-activity method, it is often difficult to make a reasonable estimate of total activity. When an asset's productive capacity varies significantly from one period to another, this method results in the best matching of expenses with revenues. In real life, when the total actual units of activity does not exactly equal the total estimated units of activity, the final year's amortization is usually adjusted so that the ending net book value is equal to the estimated residual value.

When the asset is purchased during the year, amortization expense is not pro-rated for the time the asset was used, because the units-of-activity method is based on actual units produced during the period rather than how long the asset was used during the period.

### Comparison of Amortization Methods

Amortization results, when other expenses are constant, can be compared as follows:

**Straight-line** gives a constant amount of amortization expense and net income in each year. **Declining-balance** results in a higher amortization expense in early years and thus lower income, but lower amortization expense in later years and thus higher income. The **units-of-activity** method varies since amortization expense depends on the actual usage of the asset each year.

Each method is acceptable since they all recognize the decline in service potential of assets in a rational and systematic manner. The choice of a method is based on the revenue pattern of each type of asset.

### Amortization and Income Tax

The Canada Revenue Agency (CRA) allows taxpayers to deduct amortization expense when calculating taxable income. For accounting purposes, a company may choose the amortization method that best matches revenue to expense. Amortization, allowed for income tax purposes, is calculated on a group basis and is called **capital cost allowance (CCA)**.

The CRA does not permit taxpayers to estimate the useful life or amortization rates of assets. It groups assets into various classes and provides maximum amortization rates for each class. It also sets the rules for partial amortization for assets purchased during a current year. CRA requires taxpayers to use the single declining-balance method on the tax return, regardless of what method is used in the financial statement to calculate amortization expense.

## Revising Periodic Amortization

**study objective 3**

Revise periodic amortization.

Amortization needs to be revised if there are changes in any of the three factors that affect amortization: the asset's cost, useful life, and residual value. Revisions are made if:
1. the asset's cost changes as a result of capital expenditures during its useful life.
2. there are impairments in the asset's market value.
3. there are changes in the estimated useful life or residual value.

### Capital Expenditures during Useful Life

**Ordinary repairs** are costs to maintain an asset's operating efficiency and expected productive life. Such repairs are usually fairly small amounts that occur frequently and are debited to Repair (or Maintenance) Expense as they occur and are called **operating expenditures**.

**Additions and improvements** are costs incurred to increase an asset's operating efficiency, productive capacity, or expected useful life. These costs are usually large and do not occur often. They increase the company's ability to produce and are capital expenditures. **Capital expenditures** are debited to the original asset account to which they relate and are amortized over the remaining life of that asset.

## Impairments

Assets are carried at cost in accordance with the cost principle. Book value of an asset is calculated when the accumulated amortization is subtracted from the cost. Market value of a long-lived asset is not normally relevant since long-lived assets are not bought for resale, but for use in operations. However, there are times when the market value of a long-lived asset falls far below its book value. This may occur when a machine becomes obsolete. If the decline in the asset's market value is permanent and its net book value is not recoverable, an **impairment loss** has occurred. The amount of the impairment loss is the amount by which the book value is greater than its market value.

For example, on December 31, 2008, the Butler Company had on its books a computer that cost $30,000. The accumulated amortization of the asset was $15,000. On that date the computer's market value was $5,000. The loss is deemed to be permanent and the net book value is not recoverable. The entry to record the loss is as follows:

| | | | |
|---|---|---|---|
| Dec. 31 | Loss on Impairment | 10,000 | |
| | Accumulated Amortization—Equipment | | 10,000 |
| | To record impairment loss on computer | | |

Note that the asset account is not used and the original cost of the asset is kept at its historical cost. The book value will reflect the market value ($30,000 - $25,000), $5,000. Also note that if the market value increases after the asset has been written down, the book value is not adjusted for the recovery in value.

## Changes in Estimated Useful Life or Residual Value

Management should periodically review its estimates of the useful life and residual value of the company's amortizable assets. This is done since these estimates may cause revision to the amortization calculations.

## Revised Amortization Calculations

Revision of amortization is a change in an estimate. The reason for this is that the original calculation of amortization is based on the best information available at that time. The revision is based on new information and only affects future periods. There is no correction of previously recorded amortization expense.

For example, the Forrester Company has an asset, bought on January 1, 2008, which cost $20,000. The asset's residual value is $4,000, and it has a useful life of 4 years. On January 1, 2010, the asset's estimated useful life was reviewed and was increased by 2 years. There was no change in the estimated residual value. The asset had been amortized using the straight-line method. The revised amortization is calculated as follows:

$$\text{Net book value on Jan. 1, 2010} = \$20,000 - [((\$20,000 - \$4,000) \div 4 \text{ yrs}) \times 2]$$
$$= \$20,000 - \$8,000$$
$$= \$12,000$$

$$\text{Net Book Value} - \text{Residual Value} = \text{Remaining Amortizable Cost at Time of Change in Estimate}$$
$$\$12,000 - \$4,000 = \$8,000$$

| Remaining Amortizable Cost at time of Change in Estimate | | Remaining Estimated Useful Life | | Revised Annual Amortization |
|---|---|---|---|---|
| $8,000 | ÷ | 4 years | = | $2,000 |

Amortization can be revised regardless of which method of amortization is used. If the units-of-activity method is used, the remaining estimate of useful life is expressed in units. If the declining-balance method is used, the revised rate would be applied to the net book value at the time of the change in estimate.

# Disposals of Property, Plant, and Equipment

**study objective 4**

Account for the disposal of property, plant, and equipment.

Property, plant, and equipment may be disposed of by retirement, sale, or exchange when an item is no longer useful to the company. Four steps are required to record the disposal of an asset.

**Step 1: Update amortization.**
If the disposal occurs within the accounting period, update for any period that is unrecorded at the date of disposal. The update period should never be more than one year, since adjusting entries should be made annually.

**Step 2: Calculate the net book value.**
Net book value must be calculated after the accumulated amortization is updated in Step 1.

**Step 3: Calculate the gain or loss**.
Gain or loss is determined by comparing the proceeds of the sale with the new book value. If the proceeds are more than the net book value, there is a gain on disposal. If the proceeds are less than the net book value, there is a loss on disposal.

**Step 4: Record the disposal**.
Recording the disposal of the asset means removing the assets from the accounts. The cost of the asset, and the accumulated amortization related to the asset, are removed by crediting the asset account and debiting the accumulated amortization account. The proceeds (if any) and the gain or loss (if any) are recorded. A gain on disposal is recorded as a credit; a loss on disposal is recorded as a debit.

### Retirement of Property, Plant, and Equipment

Disposal by retirement occurs when an asset is at the end of its useful life and the company no longer needs it. If the asset is fully amortized, the entry is a debit to the Accumulated Amortization account and a credit to the Asset account. If the asset is retired before it is fully amortized and no scrap or residual value is received, a loss on disposal occurs.

For example, on November 30, the Perez Company retires a machine with a cost of $24,000 and accumulated amortization of $22,000 to the date of disposal. The machine has no residual value and Perez Company does not receive any proceeds from the disposal of the asset. The entry to record the disposal is as follows:

| | | | |
|---|---|---|---|
| Nov. 30 | Accumulated Amortization—Equipment | 22,000 | |
| | Loss on Disposal | 2,000 | |
| | Equipment | | 24,000 |
| | To record retirement of machine at a loss | | |

### Sale of Property, Plant, and Equipment

In a disposal by sale, the asset's net book value is compared with the proceeds received from the sale. If the sale proceeds exceed the net book value, a gain on disposal occurs. If the sale proceeds are less than the asset's net book value, a loss on disposal occurs.

**Gain on Disposal.** For example, on September 30, Perez Company sells a machine, with a cost of $24,000 and accumulated amortization of $22,000 to the date of disposal, for $5,000 cash. The sale results in a $3,000 gain to Perez because the proceeds ($5,000) are greater than the net book value ($2,000) of the machine. The journal entry to record the sale is:

| Sept. 30 | Cash | 5,000 | |
| | Accumulated Amortization—Machine | 22,000 | |
| | Machine | | 24,000 |
| | Gain on Disposal | | 3,000 |
| | To record sale of machine at a gain | | |

**Loss on Disposal.** For example, on September 30, Perez Company sells the machine described above for $500 cash. The sale results in a $1,500 loss because the proceeds ($500) are $1,500 less than the net book value ($2,000) of the machine. The journal entry to record the sale is:

| Sept. 30 | Cash | 500 | |
| | Accumulated Amortization—Machine | 22,000 | |
| | Loss on Disposal | 1,500 | |
| | Machine | | 24,000 |
| | To record sale of machine at a loss | | |

### Exchanges of Property, Plant, and Equipment

Sometimes an old asset may be exchanged for a new asset. An old asset may be traded in for a new one and a trade-in allowance may be granted toward the purchase price of the new asset. Cash may also be involved. The new asset is seen as being purchased for cash plus the value of the old asset.

The accounting for exchange transactions depends on whether the exchange is a **monetary** or **non-monetary** exchange of assets. A monetary exchange occurs when similar assets are exchanged and a significant amount of cash is included. A non-monetary exchange occurs when assets are exchanged, with little or no cash involved in the transaction.

**Monetary Exchanges of Assets.** A monetary exchange occurs when a significant amount of cash is involved in the transaction. The exchange is viewed as both a sale of the old asset and a purchase of the new asset. The new asset is recorded at the fair market value of the asset given up plus any cash paid (or less any cash received). Gains or losses are realized when book value is compared with market value of the asset given up. Gains and losses are determined just as they are for the sale of property, plant, and equipment.

**Non-monetary Exchanges of Assets.** In a non-monetary exchange, little or no cash is involved in the transaction. Generally, non-monetary exchanges of long-lived assets are accounted for in the same way as monetary exchanges of long-lived assets. However, if the transaction does not change the business operations, or the fair values cannot be determined, the new asset is recorded at the net book value of the old asset given up plus any cash paid (or less any cash received). Net book value is used because the new asset is simply substituted or swapped for the old asset. No gain or loss is recorded in the exchange.

## Natural Resources

**Natural resources** consist of standing timber and underground deposits of oil, gas, and minerals. These assets are frequently called **wasting assets** because they are physically extracted in mining, cutting, or pumping operations and can only be replaced by an act of nature.

The cost of a natural resource can also be increased by future removal and site restoration cleanup costs. These costs, known as asset retirement obligations, can be significant.

study objective 5

Calculate and record amortization of natural resources.

## Cost

The cost of acquiring a natural resource is determined the same way as the cost of property, plant, and equipment. It can also be increased by future removal and site restoration cleanup costs, which are large. These costs, known as retirement obligations, are usually required to return the resource as closely as possible to its natural state at the end of its useful life.

## Amortization

The units-of-activity method is generally used to calculate the amortization of wasting assets. Since natural resource amortization is generally a function of the units extracted during a given period, the amortizable cost per unit of product is multiplied by the number of units extracted to calculate amortization expense. The formula for calculating amortization expense is the same as the units-of-activity method illustrated earlier.

However, the entry to record amortization of the natural resource is different from the entry for the units-of-activity method. For example, the Nubal Mining Company purchased a mine for $4 million. It has calculated its amortization for the year ended December 31, 2010, to be $300,000 based on the units extracted from its mining activity. The entry to record the amortization of Nubal for the period is as follows:

| | | | |
|---|---|---|---|
| Dec. 31 | Inventory | 300,000 | |
| |     Accumulated Amortization—Mines | | 300,000 |
| |     To record amortization expense on mines | | |

All costs of extracting the natural resource are recorded as inventory. When the resource extracted is sold, the inventory is reduced and the cost of goods sold is recorded and matched with the period's revenue.

Amortizable cost per unit of a natural resource may be revised if new information becomes available and the estimates need to be revised. Natural resources are also reviewed and tested for impairment whenever circumstances make this appropriate.

## Disposal of Natural Resources

Before disposal of the natural resource, the amortization must be recorded to the date of disposal. The proceeds are recorded, the cost and the accumulated amortization of the natural resource are removed, and any gain or loss is recorded.

# Intangible Assets

**study objective 6**

Identify the basic accounting issues for intangible assets.

Intangible assets provide future benefits through the special rights, privileges, and competitive advantage they convey. They have no physical characteristics and may arise from the following sources:
1. Government grants such as patents, copyrights, contracts, trademarks, and trade names
2. An acquisition of another business in which the purchase price includes a payment for goodwill
3. Private monopolistic arrangements arising from contractual agreements such as franchises and leases

# Accounting for Intangible Assets

Intangible assets are recorded at cost, which includes all costs of acquisition and other costs necessary to make the intangible ready for its intended use. Intangibles may have a limited useful life or an indefinite useful life. If an intangible asset has a limited useful life, its amortizable cost (cost minus residual value) is allocated over the shorter of its estimated useful life or its legal life. The useful life is usually shorter than the legal life, so useful life is most often used as the amortization period.

Amortization of intangibles is usually done on a straight-line basis. If an intangible asset has an indefinite life, it is not amortized. However, the asset cost is reviewed and tested for impairment whenever circumstances make this appropriate. If the asset's market value permanently declines below its book value, an impairment has occurred. An impairment loss should be recorded and the intangible asset written down to its market value. At disposal, the book value of the intangible asset is eliminated, and any gain or loss is recorded.

# Intangible Assets with Limited Lives

### Patents
A patent is an exclusive right that enables the recipient to manufacture, sell, or otherwise control an invention for a period of 20 years from the date of the application. The initial cost of a patent is the cash or cash equivalent price paid when the patent is acquired. The cost of the patent should be amortized over its legal life (20 years) or useful life, whichever is shorter.

If there is an infringement of a patent, the legal costs incurred to successfully defend it are added to the Patent account and amortized over the patent's remaining useful life. The legal costs are considered necessary to prove the patent's validity.

### Copyrights
Copyrights give the owner the exclusive right to reproduce and sell an artistic or published work. Copyrights in Canada extend for the life of the creator plus 50 years. The cost of a copyright includes the cost of acquiring and defending it and should be amortized over its legal life or its useful life, whichever is shorter. Generally its useful life is shorter than its legal life.

### Research and Development Costs
Research and development (R&D) costs are not intangible assets in themselves, but R&D costs lead to patents and copyrights, new processes, and new products. R&D costs bring up two accounting problems: (1) How are costs determined for specific projects? (2) How do you know the when future benefits will occur and how much they will be?

Accounting distinguishes between research costs and development costs. Research is planned activity to gain new knowledge and understanding. All research costs should be expensed when incurred. Development is the use of research findings and knowledge for a plan or design. Development costs with reasonably certain future benefits can be capitalized.

### Deferred Costs and Other Intangible Assets
Some companies use the term "Deferred Costs" to classify items like customer lists, non-competition agreements, and sports contracts. Other companies use the term "Other Assets" to classify these items. The accounting for these items is beyond the scope of this text.

## Intangible Assets with Indefinite Lives

Trademarks and trade names, franchises and licences, and goodwill are intangible assets with indefinite lives. Sometimes they have limited lives and should be amortized over the shorter of their legal or useful lives.

### Trademarks and Trade Names

A trademark or trade name is a word, phrase, jingle, or symbol that identifies a particular enterprise or product. Because they create immediate product identification, they help the sale of a product or service. In most cases, companies renew their trademarks or trade names every 15 years, so the trademark or trade name may have an indefinite useful life for as long as it remains marketable.

### Franchises and Licences

A franchise is a contractual arrangement between a franchisor and a franchisee. The franchisor gives the franchisee permission to sell certain products, offer specific services, or use certain trademarks or trade names.

Another type of franchise, granted by a government body, permits the enterprise to use public property in performing its services. These operating rights are called **licences**. An example of licences is the use of airwaves for radio and TV broadcasting.

All costs that can be identified with the acquisition of the franchise or licence should be recognized. Accounting for these costs depends on the useful life. Annual payments made by franchise agreement to the franchisor in proportion to sales are called royalties.

### Goodwill

Goodwill is the value of all favourable attributes that relate to a company. These include exceptional management, desirable location, good customer relations, skilled employees, high-quality products, fair pricing policies, and harmonious relations with labour unions.

Goodwill cannot be sold individually as it is part of the business as a whole. It is recorded only when there is a purchase of an entire business. It is recorded as the excess of cost (purchase price) over the fair market value of the net assets (assets less liabilities) acquired. Goodwill has an indefinite life and is not amortized. However, it must be tested regularly for impairment since its subjective value can change easily.

# Statement Presentation and Analysis

## Presentation

**study objective 7**

Illustrate the reporting and analysis of long-lived assets.

Property, plant, equipment, and natural resources are combined and reported on the balance sheet as "property, plant, and equipment" or "capital assets." Intangible assets are normally listed separately, following property, plant, and equipment. Goodwill must be disclosed separately. For assets that are amortized, balances and the accumulated amortization should be disclosed on the balance sheet or in the notes to the financial statements. The amortization methods used should be described and the amount of amortization expense for the period should also be disclosed. Impairment losses, if any, should be shown on a separate line on the income statement, with details disclosed in a note to the financial statement.

## Analysis

Two ratios to assess the profitability of total assets will be used: asset turnover and return on assets.

### Asset Turnover

The asset turnover ratio indicates how efficiently a company uses its assets. It shows the dollars of sales produced for each dollar invested in assets. It is calculated as follows:

$$\text{Net Sales} \div \text{Average Total Assets} = \text{Asset Turnover}$$

### Return on Assets

The return on assets ratio measures overall profitability. It focuses on net income, showing the amount of net income generated by each dollar invested in assets. It is calculated as follows:

$$\text{Net Income} \div \text{Average Total Assets} = \text{Return on Assets}$$

# Demonstration Problem (SO 1, 2, & 4)

On January 1, 2009, Hume Company purchases a machine that has a cash price of $7,000, freight charges of $250, insurance during transit of $50, assembly costs of $150, and a licence of $35 per year. Hume amortizes the machine using the straight-line method based on a five-year useful life with an estimated residual value of $700.

### Instructions

(a) Prepare the entry for the purchase on January 1, 2009.
(b) Prepare the entry to record amortization to December 31, 2009.
(c) Using the double declining-balance method, prepare an amortization schedule using the same information above.
(d) Using the declining-balance schedule prepared in (c), record the sale of the asset on December 31, 2010, if the asset were sold for $5,000 cash.

# Solution to Demonstration Problem

| General Journal | | | | JI |
|---|---|---|---|---|
| **Date** | **Account Titles and Explanation** | | **Debit** | **Credit** |
| (a) | | | | |
| 2009 | | | | |
| Jan.    1 | Equipment | | 7,450 | |
| | Licence Expense | | 35 | |
| | Cash | | | 7,485 |
| | ($7,000 + $250 + $50 + $150) | | | |
| | | | | |
| (b) | | | | |
| Dec.    31 | Amortization Expense | | 1,350 | |
| | Accumulated Amortization—Equipment | | | 1,350 |
| | [($7,450 – $700) ÷ 5] | | | |

(c) Calculation of double-declining rate:
    Straight-line rate = 100% ÷ 5 = 20%
    Double declining-balance rate = 20% x 2 = 40%

**Double Declining-Balance Amortization Schedule**

| Year | Net Book Value Beginning of the Year | Amortization Rate | Amortization Expense | End of Year Accumulated Amortization | End of Year Net Book Value |
|---|---|---|---|---|---|
| 2009 | $7,450 | 40% | $2,980 | $2,980 | $4,470 |
| 2010 | 4,470 | 40% | 1,788 | 4,768 | 2,682 |
| 2011 | 2,682 | 40% | 1,073 | 5,841 | 1,609 |
| 2012 | 1,609 | 40% | 644 | 6,485 | 965 |
| 2013 | 965 | 40% | 265* | 6,750 | 700 |

*Amortization expense for 2013 is $265 and not 40% of $965 because the asset cannot be amortized below its residual value.

(d)
```
2010
Dec. 31   Cash                                          5,000
          Accumulated Amortization—Equipment            4,768
              Equipment                                           7,450
              Gain on Sale of Equipment                           2,318
```

# Review Questions and Exercises

## Multiple Choice

Circle the letter that best answers each of the following statements.

1. (SO 1 & 6) All of the following are descriptions of property, plant, and equipment except:

   a. long-lived assets.
   b. fixed assets.
   c. intangible assets.
   d. capital assets.

2. (SO 1) Property, plant, and equipment are often subdivided into four groups. Which of the following would not be classified as property, plant, and equipment?

   a. Land
   b. Land Improvements
   c. Supplies
   d. Buildings

3. (SO 1) Plato Company acquired land with a purchase price of $150,000. Legal fees on acquisition were $6,000. Plato also incurred the following costs: demolition and removal of an old building, $4,000; grading and filling of land, $3,000; parking lot layout, $4,000. The land should be recorded at:

   a. $167,000.
   b. $150,000.
   c. $157,000.
   d. $163,000.

4. (SO 1) Land improvements include all of the following costs except:

   a. land survey.
   b. driveways.
   c. parking lots.
   d. fencing.

5. (SO 1) Mackenna Company purchased a delivery truck and incurred the following costs:

   | | |
   |---|---|
   | Cash price | $30,000 |
   | Painting of logo | 600 |
   | Motor vehicle licence | 75 |
   | Two-year accident insurance policy | 700 |

What amount should be recorded as the cost of the delivery truck?

a. $30,000
b. $30,600
c. $30,675
d. $31,300

6. (SO 1) Esmay Industries purchased real estate for $365,000. It paid $65,000 and took a mortgage in the amount of $300,000. Legal fees of $4,000 cash were also paid for the purchase. The real estate appraisal of the land was $375,000 and of the building was $200,000. The amount recorded in the Land account on recording the purchase is:

a. $300,000.
b. $365,000.
c. $240,652.
d. $375,000.

7. (SO 2) The factor that is not relevant in calculating amortization is:

a. replacement value.
b. cost.
c. residual value.
d. useful life.

8. (SO 2) Using the straight-line method, amortization expense is calculated as:

a. (Cost ÷ Useful Life) - Residual Value.
b. (Cost + Residual Value) ÷ Useful Life.
c. (Cost - Residual Value) ÷ Useful Life.
d. (Cost ÷ Useful Life) + Residual Value.

9. (SO 2) Bruno Company purchased equipment on January 1, 2008, at a total invoice cost of $280,000; additional costs of $5,000 for freight and $25,000 for installation were incurred. The equipment has an estimated residual value of $9,000 and an estimated useful life of five years. The amount of accumulated amortization at December 31, 2009, if the straight-line method of amortization is used, is:

a. $ 98,000.
b. $ 19,000.
c. $120,400.
d. $124,000.

10. (SO 2) Espinoza Enterprises purchased a truck for $27,000 on January 1, 2010. The truck will have an estimated residual value of $2,000 at the end of five years. Using the units-of-activity method, the accumulated amortization at December 31, 2011, can be calculated as:

a. ($27,000 ÷ Total Estimated Activity) x Units of Activity for 2010.
b. ($25,000 ÷ Total Estimated Activity) x Units of Activity for 2011.
c. ($27,000 ÷ Total Estimated Activity) x Units of Activity for 2010 and 2011.
d. ($25,000 ÷ Total Estimated Activity) x Units of Activity for 2010 and 2011.

11. (SO 2) The Newman Company purchased a machine on January 1, 2010, for $350,000. The machine has an estimated useful life of five years and a residual value of $50,000. The machine is being amortized using the double declining-balance method. The net book value at December 31, 2011, is:

 a. $126,000.
 b. $158,000.
 c. $170,000.
 d. $224,000.

12. (SO 2) The amortization method that normally charges the same amount to expense every year is:

 a. double declining-balance.
 b. capital cost allowance.
 c. straight-line.
 d. units-of-activity.

13. (SO 2) The amortizable cost of an asset equals:

 a. market value minus residual value.
 b. cost minus accumulated amortization.
 c. cost minus residual value.
 d. cost minus amortization expense.

14. (SO 2) Amortization, for income tax purposes, is calculated using which of the following amortization methods?

 a. Double declining-balance
 b. Single declining-balance
 c. Straight-line
 d. Units-of-activity

15. (SO 2) The entry to record amortization expense:

 a. decreases owner's equity and assets.
 b. decreases net income and increases liabilities.
 c. decreases assets and liabilities.
 d. decreases assets and increases liabilities.

16. (SO 3) Santana Company purchased a machine on January 1, 2011, for $8,000 with an estimated residual value of $2,000 and an estimated useful life of eight years. On January 1, 2013, Santana estimated that the machine will last 12 years from the date of purchase. The residual value is still estimated at $2,000. Using the straight-line method, the new annual amortization will be:

 a. $450.
 b. $500.
 c. $600.
 d. $667.

17. (SO 3) Which of the following would be considered an ordinary repair?

    a. Constructing a new wing on a building
    b. Performing a major motor overhaul on a new truck
    c. Painting buildings
    d. Replacing a stairway with an escalator

18. (SO 3) Additions and Improvements are:

    a. operating expenditures.
    b. debited to an appropriate asset account when they increase useful life.
    c. debited to accumulated amortization when they do not increase useful life.
    d. debited to an appropriate asset account when they do not increase useful life.

19. (SO 3) Impairments occur when:

    a. an asset's market value falls below its book value.
    b. the market value falls but increases in future years.
    c. there is a permanent decline in the market value of the asset.
    d. the asset loses value through obsolescence.

20. (SO 4) A long-lived asset may be disposed of by:

    a. retirement.
    b. sale.
    c. exchange.
    d. all of the above.

21. (SO 4) Equipment costing $27,000 was purchased on January 1, 2006. It was amortized using the straight-line method based on a nine-year life with no residual value. On June 30, 2013, the equipment was discarded with no cash proceeds. What gain or loss should be recognized on the retirement?

    a. No gain or loss
    b. $6,000 loss
    c. $4,500 loss
    d. $3,000 gain

22. (SO 4) On January 1, Gardner Company sold a machine that had a net book value of $7,500 for $8,000 cash. The entry by Gardner Company on January 1 will include a:

    a. debit to Loss on Disposal.
    b. credit to Loss on Disposal.
    c. debit to Gain on Disposal.
    d. debit to Cash.

23. (SO 5) Natural resources include all of the following except:

    a. standing timber.
    b. land improvements.
    c. oil deposits.
    d. mineral deposits.

24. (SO 5) Abelard Company expects to extract 15 million tonnes of coal from a mine that cost $25 million. If no residual value is expected and 3 million tonnes are mined in the first year, the entry to record amortization in the first year will include a:

    a.  debit to Accumulated Amortization of $3,000,000.
    b.  credit to Amortization Expense of $5,000,000.
    c.  credit to Accumulated Amortization of $5,000,000.
    d.  debit to Amortization Expense of $1,800,000.

25. (SO 6) All of the following are intangible assets except:

    a.  franchises.
    b.  copyrights.
    c.  accounts receivable.
    d.  goodwill.

26. (SO 6) A purchased patent has a remaining legal life of 15 years. It should:

    a.  be expensed in the year of acquisition.
    b.  be amortized over 15 years regardless of its useful life.
    c.  be amortized over its useful life if less than 15 years.
    d.  not be amortized.

27. (SO 6) Eloise Company incurred $350,000 of research costs in its laboratory to develop a patent granted on January 1, 2013. On July 31, 2013, Eloise paid $52,000 for legal fees to successfully defend the patent. The total amount debited to Patents through July 31, 2013, should be:

    a.  $350,000.
    b.  $52,000.
    c.  $402,000.
    d.  $298,000.

28. (SO 6) Goodwill from the acquisition of a business enterprise:

    a.  should be expensed in the year of acquisition.
    b.  is an asset that is subject to amortization.
    c.  is an intangible asset.
    d.  is granted by the federal government.

29. (SO 7) The balances of the major classes of property, plant, and equipment and accumulated amortization should be disclosed:

    a.  on bank loan applications.
    b.  in the notes to the balance sheet.
    c.  in the notes to the financial statement.
    d.  on the income tax return.

30. (SO 7) When calculating the asset turnover ratio, we divide net sales total by:

    a.  total equity.
    b.  average liabilities.
    c.  total revenue.
    d.  average total assets.

## Matching

Match each term with its definition by writing the appropriate letter in the space provided.

| **Terms** | **Definitions** |
|---|---|
| ____ 1. Operating Expenditures | a. An amortization method that applies a constant rate to the declining net book value of the asset over the useful life of the asset. |
| ____ 2. Declining-balance method | b. Expenditures that are immediately charged against revenues as expenses. |
| ____ 3. Natural resources | c. An exclusive right that enables the recipient to manufacture, sell, or otherwise control an invention for a period of 20 years from the date of application. |
| ____ 4. Cash equivalent price | |
| ____ 5. Additions and improvements | d. An amortization method in which the decline in service potential is attributable to activity rather than time. |
| ____ 6. Ordinary repairs | e. An amount equal to the fair market value of the asset given up, if known; otherwise, the fair market value of the asset received. |
| ____ 7. Units-of-activity method | f. Costs incurred to increase the operating efficiency, productive capacity, or expected productive life of property, plant, or equipment. |
| ____ 8. Straight-line method | |
| ____ 9. Patent | g. Expenditures to maintain the operating efficiency and productive life of the asset. |
| ____ 10. Intangible assets | h. The amount paid for a business in excess of the net identifiable assets. |
| ____ 11. Copyright | i. An amortization method where the amortization expense for the period is the same throughout the service life of the asset. |
| ____ 12. Amortizable cost | |
| ____ 13. Franchise | j. Rights, privileges, and competitive advantages that result from the ownership of long-lived assets that do not possess physical substance. |
| ____ 14. Goodwill | k. Expenditures that may lead to new products, processes, patents, and copyrights. |
| ____ 15. Trademark | l. Long-lived assets that consist of standing timber and underground deposits of oil, gas, and minerals. |
| ____ 16. Research and development costs | |

____ 17. Capital cost allowance

    m.  A word, phrase, or symbol that distinguishes or identifies a particular enterprise or product.

    n.  A right granted by the federal government giving the owner the exclusive right to reproduce and sell an artistic or published work.

    o.  A contractual agreement granting rights to sell certain products, render specific services, or use certain trademarks within a certain area.

    p.  The declining-balance method used to amortize property, plant, and equipment as specified for income tax purposes.

    q.  The cost of a long-lived asset less its residual value.

## Exercises

**E9-1**    (SO 1) During 2010, Bergson Company had the following property and equipment transactions:

Jan.    1    Purchased a bus for company tours. The bus had a purchase price of $123,000, plus costs of $500 for delivery charges, $500 for insurance during transit to the company, $4,000 for painting and lettering, $3,000 for motor vehicle licence, and $6,000 for accident insurance for two years. Bergson Company paid $20,000 in cash and signed a Note Payable for the balance.

July    1    Purchased a factory machine and some office equipment for a total of $12,000 cash. The fair value of the factory machine was $9,000 and the fair value of the office equipment was $15,000.

**Instructions**

Journalize the transactions. Explanations are not necessary.

| | General Journal | | J1 |
|---|---|---|---|
| **Date** | **Account Titles** | **Debit** | **Credit** |
| 2010 | | | |
| | | | |
| | | | |
| | | | |
| | | | |
| | | | |
| | | | |
| | | | |
| | | | |
| | | | |
| | | | |
| | | | |
| | | | |
| | | | |
| | | | |
| | | | |
| | | | |
| | | | |
| | | | |

**E9-2**    (SO 1) On September 1, the Borzoa Company purchased real estate with a down payment of $69,000 cash and a mortgage of $300,000. The market value of the land was $375,000 and the building was $200,000.

### Instructions
(a) Calculate the cost that should be allocated to each asset purchased.
(b) Record the purchase of the real estate.

**E9-3**    (SO 2) On January 1, 2009, Dewey Company purchased computer equipment for $150,000. The computer equipment is estimated to have a $30,000 residual value after its four-year useful life.

## Instructions
Fill in the appropriate amounts concerning the amortization of the computer under the amortization methods identified below.

**Straight-Line Method**

| | Calculation | | | End of Year | |
|---|---|---|---|---|---|
| Year | Net Book Value Beginning of the Year | x Amortization Rate | = Amortization Expense | Accumulated Amortization | Net Book Value |
| 2009 | | | | | |
| 2010 | | | | | |
| 2011 | | | | | |

**Double Declining-Balance Method**

| | Calculation | | | End of Year | |
|---|---|---|---|---|---|
| Year | Net Book Value Beginning of the Year | x Amortization Rate | = Amortization Expense | Accumulated Amortization | Net Book Value |
| 2009 | | | | | |
| 2010 | | | | | |
| 2011 | | | | | |

**E9-4**    (SO 4) During 2010, LeBarge Company had the following transactions related to its property, plant, and equipment. LeBarge Company normally records amortization expense at the end of the annual fiscal year.

Jan.   1   A delivery truck costing $17,500, with accumulated amortization of $6,500, is destroyed in an accident. The insurance company pays LeBarge $13,000.

July   1   Sold machinery costing $17,000 for $2,200 cash. The machinery had accumulated amortization of $12,000 at December 31, 2009, based on annual amortization of $2,000 per year.

Dec.  31   Retired a machine with a cost of $20,000 and accumulated amortization of $18,000 to the end of 2009. The machine has been amortized on the straight-line basis for nine years, with no estimated residual value. The machine has been used in the business throughout the entire year 2010 and is being retired at the end of the year.

## Instructions
Journalize the transactions. Explanations are not necessary.

| General Journal | | | JI |
|---|---|---|---|
| **Date** | **Account Titles** | **Debit** | **Credit** |
| 2010 | | | |
| | | | |
| | | | |
| | | | |
| | | | |
| | | | |
| | | | |
| | | | |
| | | | |
| | | | |
| | | | |
| | | | |
| | | | |
| | | | |
| | | | |
| | | | |
| | | | |
| | | | |
| | | | |
| | | | |
| | | | |
| | | | |
| | | | |
| | | | |
| | | | |
| | | | |
| | | | |
| | | | |
| | | | |
| | | | |
| | | | |
| | | | |
| | | | |

**E9-5** (SO 6) On December 31, 2010, the intangible asset section of Mill Company's balance sheet was:

| | | |
|---|---:|---:|
| Patents | $210,000 | |
| Less: Accumulated amortization | 13,000 | $197,000 |
| Franchise | 120,000 | |
| Less: Accumulated amortization | 48,000 | 72,000 |
| Copyrights | 60,000 | |
| Less: Accumulated amortization | 48,000 | 12,000 |
| Total intangibles | | $281,000 |

Mill owns two patents: one purchased for $50,000 on January 1, 2010, with a total useful life of 10 years, and the other purchased for $160,000 on January 1, 2010, with a total useful life of 20 years. The franchise was obtained on January 1, 2005, for $120,000 and is being amortized over its contract life of 15 years. The copyrights were also capitalized on January 1, 2007, at a cost of $60,000 and are being amortized over five years. During 2011, Mill purchased a patent on July 1 at a cost of $72,000. This patent has an estimated economic life of 12 years from July 1, 2011.

### Instructions
Prepare the December 31, 2011, intangible assets section of Mill Company's balance sheet. Show all calculations for each intangible asset.

**MILL COMPANY**
**Partial Balance Sheet**
**December 31, 2011**

**E9-6**     (SO 7) The Samora Company has given you the following information from its financial statements for the year ended December 31, 2011.

| | |
|---|---|
| Total Net Sales | $1,220,567 |
| Assets at beginning of year | $ 768,000 |
| Assets at the ending of year | $ 694,762 |
| Net Income for the year | $ 40,829 |

Calculate the following ratios:
(a) The asset turnover for the year.
(b) The return on assets for the year.

_____

_____

_____

_____

_____

_____

_____

_____

_____

_____

_____

_____

_____

# Solutions to Review Questions and Exercises

## Multiple Choice

1. (c)  Intangible assets are not included in property, plant, and equipment because they do not have physical substance. (a) Long-lived assets, (b) fixed assets, and (d) capital assets all refer to tangible assets.

2. (c)  Property, plant, and equipment are subdivided into four classes: (i) Land, (ii) Land improvements, (iii) Buildings, and (iv) Equipment. Supplies is classified as a current asset.

3. (d)  The acquisition of land will consist of the purchase price ($150,000), lawyer's fee ($6,000), demolition and removal costs of an old building ($4,000), and grading and filling ($3,000), for a total of $163,000.

4. (a)  Land survey costs are recorded in the Land account. Land improvements include driveways, parking lots, and fencing.

5. (b)  The cost of a long-lived asset consists of all expenditures necessary to acquire the asset and make it ready for its intended use ($30,000 + $600 = $30,600). The payment for the licence is an annual recurring operating expenditure. The insurance premium is recorded as prepaid insurance and is expensed over its two-year life.

6. (c)  The basket purchase of real estate was made at a total cost of $369,000. The total cost allocated to the Land account is calculated based on the appraisal of the land and the building. It is calculated as follows:

$$\frac{\$375,000}{\$575,000} \times \$369,000 = \$240,652$$

7. (a)  Replacement value is not relevant in calculating amortization.

8. (c)  The formula for calculating amortization expense under the straight-line method is (Cost - Residual Value) ÷ Useful Life.

9. (c)  The cost of the equipment is $310,000 (the invoice cost of $280,000, freight costs of $5,000, and installation costs of $25,000). The annual amortization is calculated as follows:

($310,000 – $9,000) ÷ 5 = $60,200 x 2 = $120,400

10. (d)  The amortizable cost is $25,000 (cost of $27,000 minus residual value of $2,000). Accumulated amortization must include the amortization expense for both 2010 and 2011.

11. (a) Annual amortization expense is calculated by multiplying the net book value at the beginning of the year by the declining-balance rate. Residual value is ignored until the end of the asset's useful life. The amortization rate is double the straight-line rate of 20% or 20% x 2 = 40%.

| Year | Net Book Value x rate | | | Amortization Expense | Net Book Value end of Year |
|------|------|---|-----|------|------|
| 2010 | $350,000 | x | 40% | = $140,000 | $210,000 |
| 2011 | $210,000 | x | 40% | = $ 84,000 | 126,000 |

12. (c) The straight-line method of amortization will normally result in the same amount of amortization expense each year.

13. (c) The amortizable cost of an asset is equal to the cost of the asset less its residual value.

14. (b) Income tax regulations require the taxpayer to use the single declining-balance method. Amortization is calculated on a class basis and is called capital cost allowance (CCA).

15. (a) The entry to record amortization expense results in a debit to Amortization Expense and a credit to Accumulated Amortization. The debit to Amortization Expense decreases net income and thus owner's equity. The credit to Accumulated Amortization increases the contra asset account, which decreases the book value of the asset to which it relates.

16. (a) To determine the new annual amortization expense, the amortizable cost is divided by the revised remaining useful life as follows:

Amortization expense for 2010: ($8,000 – $2,000) ÷ 8 = $750

Net book value at end of 2011: $8,000 – (2 x $750) = $6,500

Remaining useful life: (12 – 2) = 10 years

Revised annual amortization for remaining 10 years: ($6,500 – $2,000) ÷ 10 = $450

17. (c) Ordinary repairs include motor tune-ups done on delivery trucks, replacing worn out tires, and painting buildings. Choices (a), (b), and (d) are additions and improvements to assets that increase the life of the asset and are considered capital expenditures.

18. (b) Additions and improvements are capital expenditures. When the expenditure increases useful life, it should be debited to an appropriate asset account.

19. (c) Impairments occur when there is a permanent decline in the asset's market value. Its net book value must also not be recoverable.

20. (d) Property, plant, and equipment may be disposed of by retirement, sale, or exchange.

21.  (c)  On June 30, 2013, the asset would have a net book value of $4,500, as calculated below:

| | |
|---|---:|
| Cost | $27,000 |
| Amortization, 2006–2012 (7 x $3,000) | (21,000) |
| Amortization, Jan. 1–June 30, 2013 (6/12 x $3,000) | (1,500) |
| Net book value, June 30, 2013 | $4,500 |

Since the asset was discarded with no cash proceeds, a loss of $4,500 should be recognized.

22.  (d)  The $8,000 cash is recorded with a debit to Cash, and since the amount of cash received is more than the asset's net book value, a gain would be recorded with a credit to Gain on Disposal.

23.  (b)  Natural resources consists of standing timber and underground deposits of oil, gas, and minerals. Land improvements are reported as tangible property, plant, and equipment.

24.  (c)  The calculation for amortization using units-of-activity method is:

$$\frac{\$25,000,000}{15,000,000} = \$1.67 \text{ and } \$1.67 \times 3,000,000 = \$5,000,000 \text{ (rounded)}$$

The entry is as follows:

| | | |
|---|---:|---:|
| Inventory | 5,000,000 | |
| Accumulated Amortization—Mine | | 5,000,000 |

25.  (c)  Intangible assets are rights, privileges, and competitive advantages that result from the ownership of long-lived assets that do not possess physical substance. They include patents, copyrights, trademarks, trade names, franchises, licences, and goodwill. Accounts receivable is a current asset.

26.  (c)  The cost of a patent should be amortized over its legal life or useful life, whichever is shorter.

27.  (b)  The research costs of $350,000 should be expensed when incurred. The legal fees ($52,000) in successfully defending the patent are debited to the Patent account.

28.  (c)  Goodwill is an intangible asset that is recognized when the purchase price to acquire an entire business exceeds the fair market value of the net assets acquired. Since goodwill does not have a legal life or an identifiable useful life, it is not subject to amortization.

29.  (c)  For assets that are amortized, the balances and accumulated amortization should be disclosed in notes to the financial statement.

30.  (d)  Asset turnover = Net sales total ÷ Average total assets.

## Matching

| | | | | | | | |
|---|---|---|---|---|---|---|---|
| 1. | b | 6. | g | 11. | n | 16. | k |
| 2. | a | 7. | d | 12. | q | 17. | p |
| 3. | l | 8. | i | 13. | o | | |
| 4. | e | 9. | c | 14. | h | | |
| 5. | f | 10. | j | 15. | m | | |

## Exercises

### E9-1

| General Journal | | | JI |
|---|---|---|---|
| **Date** | **Account Titles** | **Debit** | **Credit** |
| 2010 | | | |
| Jan. 1 | Bus | 128,000 | |
| | Licence Expense | 3,000 | |
| | Prepaid Insurance | 6,000 | |
| | Cash | | 20,000 |
| | Notes Payable | | 117,000 |
| | | | |
| July 1 | Factory Machinery | 4,500 | |
| | Office Equipment | 7,500 | |
| | Cash | | 12,000 |

### E9-2

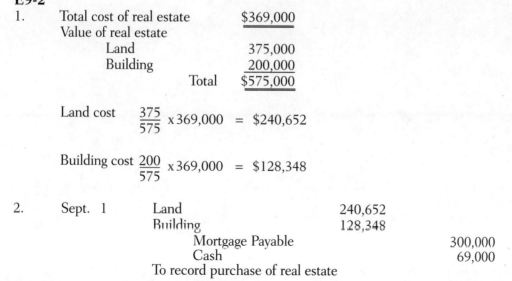

1.  | Total cost of real estate | | $369,000 |

Value of real estate
| | |
|---|---|
| Land | 375,000 |
| Building | 200,000 |
| Total | $575,000 |

Land cost  $\dfrac{375}{575} \times 369{,}000 = \$240{,}652$

Building cost  $\dfrac{200}{575} \times 369{,}000 = \$128{,}348$

2.  Sept. 1
| | | |
|---|---|---|
| Land | 240,652 | |
| Building | 128,348 | |
| Mortgage Payable | | 300,000 |
| Cash | | 69,000 |
| To record purchase of real estate | | |

E9-3

**Straight-Line Method**

|  | Calculation | | | End of Year | |
|---|---|---|---|---|---|
| Year | Amortizable Cost | x Amortization Rate | = Amortization Expense | Accumulated Amortization | Net Book Value |
| 2009 | $120,000 | 25% | $30,000 | $30,000 | $90,000 |
| 2010 | 120,000 | 25% | 30,000 | 60,000 | 60,000 |
| 2011 | 120,000 | 25% | 30,000 | 90,000 | 30,000 |

**Double Declining-Balance Method**

|  | Calculation | | | End of Year | |
|---|---|---|---|---|---|
| Year | Net Book Value at the Beginning of the Year | x Amortization Rate | = Amortization Expense | Accumulated Amortization | Net Book Value |
| 2009 | $150,000 | 50% | $75,000 | $ 75,000 | $75,000 |
| 2010 | 75,000 | 50% | 37,500 | 112,500 | 37,500 |
| 2011 | 37,500 | 50% | 7,500* | 120,000 | 30,000* |

*Amortization stops when the asset's book value equals its residual value.

E9-4

| | General Journal | | JI |
|---|---|---|---|
| **Date** | **Account Titles** | **Debit** | **Credit** |
| 2010 | | | |
| Jan. 1 | Cash | 13,000 | |
| | Accumulated Amortization—Truck | 6,500 | |
| | Truck | | 17,500 |
| | Gain on disposal | | 2,000 |
| | | | |
| July 1 | Amortization Expense | 1,000 | |
| | Accumulated Amortization—Machinery | | 1,000 |
| | | | |
| 1 | Cash | 2,200 | |
| | Accumulated Amortization—Machinery | 13,000 | |
| | Loss on Disposal | 1,800 | |
| | Machinery | | 17,000 |
| | | | |
| Dec. 31 | Amortization Expense | 2,000 | |
| | Accumulated Amortization—Machine | | 2,000 |
| | | | |
| 31 | Accumulated Amortization—Machine | 20,000 | |
| | Machine | | 20,000 |

E9-5

---

**MILL COMPANY**
**Partial Balance Sheet**
**December 31, 2011**

---

Intangible assets:

| | | |
|---|---|---|
| Patents | $282,000 | |
| Less: Accumulated amortization | 29,000 | $253,000* |
| Franchise | 120,000 | |
| Less: Accumulated amortization | 56,000 | 64,000** |
| Copyrights | 60,000 | |
| Less: Accumulated amortization | 60,000 | 0 |
| Total intangibles | | $317,000 |

Calculations:
*Patents:

| | | |
|---|---|---|
| $50,000, | Jan. 1, 2010, 10 yrs, amortization to date = | $10,000 |
| + 160,000, | Jan. 1, 2010, 20 yrs, amortization to date = | 16,000 |
| + 72,000, | July 1, 2006, 12 yrs, amortization to date = | 3,000 |
| $ 282,000, | amortization to date | 29,000 |

**Franchise:

$120,000,  Jan. 1, 2005, 15 yrs, amortization to date =     $56,000
(Accumulated amortization: $8,000 x 7 years)

Copyrights:

$60,000,  Jan. 1, 2007, 5 yrs, amortization to date =     $60,000
(Accumulated amortization: $12,000 x 5 years)

E9-6

| | |
|---|---|
| Total Net Sales | $1,220,567 |
| Assets at beginning of year | $ 768,000 |
| Assets at the ending of year | $ 694,762 |
| Net Income for the year | $ 40,829 |

1. The asset turnover for the year
    Net Sales ÷ Average Total Assets = Asset Turnover
    $1,220,567 ÷ [($768,000 + $694,762) ÷ 2] = 1.67

2. The return on assets for the year
    Net Income ÷ Average Total Assets = Return on Assets
    $40,829 ÷ [($768,000 + $694,762) ÷ 2] = 5%

chapter 10
# Current Liabilities

## study objectives >>

After studying this chapter, you should be able to:
1. Account for definitely determinable liabilities.
2. Account for estimated liabilities.
3. Account for contingencies.
4. Prepare the current liabilities section of the balance sheet.
5. Calculate the payroll for a pay period (Appendix 10A).

# Preview of Chapter 10

Every company has current liabilities. A current liability is a debt that has two features: (1) it is likely to be paid within one year, (2) it will be paid from existing current assets or by creating other current liabilities. We will explain current liabilities in this chapter. Long-term liabilities will be explained in Chapter 15. This chapter is organized as follows:

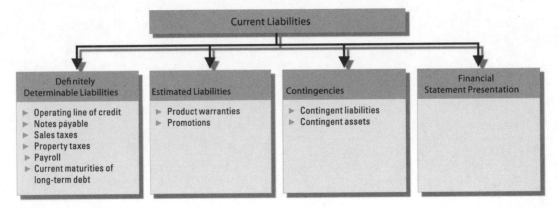

# Definitely Determinable Liabilities

Liabilities are described as definitely determinable, estimable, or contingent. A definitely determinable liability is one with a known amount, payee, and due date. Examples of definitely determinable current liabilities include bank indebtedness from operating lines of credit, notes payable, accounts payable, sales taxes payable, unearned revenue, and current maturities of long-term debt. Also included in this category are property taxes, payroll, and interest which may be accrued.

## Operating Line of Credit

An operating line of credit is a pre-authorization from the bank to borrow money, up to a pre-set limit, when it is needed. It is repayable upon request by the bank. Most companies borrow money, as needed, from the bank to meet short-term cash shortfalls.

A line of credit makes it very easy for a company to borrow money. The bank covers all cheques written by the company in excess of the company's bank account balance, up to the approved credit limit. The amount is a bank overdraft and represents a liability of the company. Interest is charged on the overdrawn amount at a floating rate. The overdraft is reported as a current liability, normally called bank indebtedness, with disclosure in the notes to the financial statements.

## Notes Payable

Notes payable are obligations in the form of written promissory notes that usually require the borrower to pay interest monthly or at maturity. Notes due for payment within one year of the balance sheet date are usually classified as current liabilities.

For example, Erhardt Company borrows $50,000 cash from Brentwood Bank on January 1, 2010, and signs a 7-month, 6% note payable. The entry to record this is as follows:

| | | | |
|---|---|---|---|
| Jan. 1 | Cash | 50,000 | |
| | Note Payable | | 50,000 |
| | To record issue of 7-month, 6% note to Brentwood Bank. | | |

During the life of the note, interest payable must be accrued as an expense and be recorded in the period when the borrowed money is used. At the end of each month Erhardt Company will record:

| | | | |
|---|---|---|---|
| Jan. 31 | Interest Expense | 250 | |
| | Interest Payable | | 250 |
| | To accrue interest for May. ($50,000 x 6% x 1/12) | | |

At maturity, Notes Payable is debited for the face value of the note, and Interest Payable is debited for accrued interest after interest is brought up to date. At the end of seven months Erhardt will record:

| | | | |
|---|---|---|---|
| Aug. 1 | Notes Payable | 50,000 | |
| | Interest Payable (7 x $250) | 1,750 | |
| | Cash | | 51,750 |
| | To record payment of note and accrued interest. | | |

## Sales Taxes

Sales taxes are expressed as a stated percentage of the sales price on goods sold to customers by a retailer. Sales taxes may take the form of Goods and Services Tax (GST), Provincial Sales Tax (PST), or Harmonized Sales Tax (HST). The entry by the retailer to record sales taxes is as follows:

| | | |
|---|---|---|
| Cash | XXXX | |
| Sales | | XXXX |
| PST Payable | | XXXX* |
| GST Payable | | XXXX |

GST is a federal tax assessed at 6% across Canada. PST* is a provincial tax whose rate varies from 0% to 10% among provinces across Canada. HST is a combination of GST and PST that is used in some provinces. Sales taxes are not an expense (or revenue) of the retailer, but must be collected and forwarded to the appropriate government. Quebec sales tax is called the QST.

If sales taxes are not rung up separately on the cash register, total receipts are divided by 100% plus the sales tax percentage to determine the sales at retail.  The difference between the amount rung up and the sales at retail is the sales tax amount that is sent to the provincial or federal government annually, quarterly, or monthly.

## Property Taxes

Property taxes, charged by municipal and provincial governments annually, are paid by businesses that own property.  Tax bills received in March are usually payable by May or later in the year.  The tax generally covers a calendar year.

Once the property tax bill has been received, the liability is recorded with the current and past month(s) expenses. For example, Maximus Company received its 2010 property tax bill in the amount of $3,600 on February 28, 2010. The entry on February 28, 2010, is as follows:

| | | | |
|---|---|---|---|
| Feb 28 | Property Tax Expense | 600 | |
| | Property Tax Payable | | 600 |
| | To record property tax expense for January and February 2010. | | |

When the business pays the annual property tax bill on April 30, 2010, the entry to record payment is:

| | | | |
|---|---|---|---|
| Apr. 30 | Property Tax Payable | 600 | |
| | Property Tax Expense ($3,600 x 2/12) | 600 | |
| | Prepaid Property Tax ($3,600 x 8/12) | 2,400 | |
| | Cash | | 3,600 |
| | To record property tax payment for 2010. | | |

After the payment, Maximus has a zero balance in its liability account but still has a prepayment. Since Maximus only makes adjusting entries annually, it would not adjust the prepaid property tax account until its year end, December 31. The entry to adjust the account on December 31 will be:

| | | | |
|---|---|---|---|
| Dec. 31 | Property Tax Expense | 2,400 | |
| | Prepaid Property Tax | | 2,400 |
| | To adjust property tax account to December 31, 2010. | | |

# Payroll

Every employer has three types of payroll liabilities related to employees' salaries or wages: (1) the net pay owed to employees, (2) employees' payroll deductions, and (3) employer payroll deductions.

Salaries and wages are often used interchangeably. The total amount of salaries/wages is called gross pay or gross earnings. Salaries are expressed as a specific amount per week, per month, or per year. Wages are based on a rate per hour or on amount per unit or product.

The amount owed to employees and recorded in salaries/wages payable is known as net pay. Net pay is calculated by deducting the employee payroll deductions from gross pay.

Payroll deductions are required by law to be withheld from employees' gross pay. Mandatory payroll deductions include federal and provincial income taxes, Canada Pension Plan (CPP) contributions, and Employment Insurance (EI) premiums. The employer may also withhold voluntary deductions for charitable donations, health insurance, pensions, union dues, and other purposes.

In addition to the amounts withheld from the employees' pay, employers must make contributions towards CPP and EI premiums. These are liabilities related to payroll. In addition, the provincial governments require employers to fund workplace health, safety, and compensation plans.

These liabilities together with items such as paid vacations and employer sponsored pensions are referred to as employee benefits. Employers match each employee's CPP contribution by an equal amount and EI contributions by 1.4 times the amount.

Until all these payments are made to employees, governments, and other third parties (e.g. United Way), they are recorded as current liabilities on the balance sheet.

The Salaries and Wages Expense are separated into liabilities—the amounts owing to employees, Wages and Salaries Payable, and the amounts owing to the government agencies and third parties. Employer payroll contributions are accounted for separately in an account normally called Employee Benefits Expense. These result in liabilities owing to government agencies and third parties.

## Current Maturities of Long-Term Debt

Current maturities of long-term debt occur when a company with long-term debt has a portion of that debt due in the current year. It is not necessary to prepare an adjusting journal entry to recognize the current debt. The current portion of the long-term debt is usually reclassified as a current liability when the balance sheet is prepared.

# Estimated Liabilities

Estimated liabilities are obligations that exist but whose amount and timing are uncertain. The company knows it will owe someone but is not sure about how much and when.

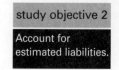

study objective 2

Account for estimated liabilities.

## Product Warranties

Product warranties are promises made by sellers to buyers to replace or repair defective products within a specified time period following the date of the sale of the item. The matching principle requires that the estimated cost of honouring product warranty contracts should be recognized as an expense in the period in which the sale occurs.

A warranty liability is an estimate of the possible number of warranty claims that will be made by customers, the expected cost to repair or replace the units, and the time in which the claims will be made. These estimates are based on the past experience of a company.

For example: The Lee Company sells 50,000 freezers and estimates that 1% will be defective and the repair cost for each defective unit would average $50. On December 31, 2010, at the year end, the company will make the following journal entries related to warranty liability.

| Dec 31 | Warranty Expense | 25,000 | |
| |     Warranty Liability | | 25,000 |
| | To accrue estimated warranty costs. | | |
| | (50,000 units x 1% x $50) | | |

Claims may be made by customers anytime within the warranty period. If at the end of December 31, 2011, warranty claims totalled $15,000, the journal entry to record customer claims honoured is:

| Dec 31 | Warranty Liability | 15,000 | |
| |     Repair Parts Inventory and/or Wages Payable | 15,000 | |
| | To record honouring of warranty contracts on 2010 sales. | | |

The credit to Repair Parts Inventory is a reduction of the asset account, inventory. The credit to Wages Payable will eventually reduce the current wages expense. The accounts may be credited separately. If, after the specified time of the warranty, the actual warranty expense is not equal to the estimated liability amount, the warranty liability should be reviewed and adjusted as required.

## Promotions

Promotions take various forms and are offered by companies to attract or keep customers. They are designed to increase sales. When promotional items result in a reduction of the selling price of an item, it should be accounted for as a decrease in revenue and not as an expense.

Similar to product warranties, promotions result in an estimated liability because companies do not know how many customers will redeem promotional offers and when the customer will do this. Therefore, promotion redemptions must be estimated in the same period that the sale is recorded. This estimate is recorded as a reduction to revenue and as a current liability.

For example: On January 1, 2010, Mega Chocolate Chip Company offered a $0.20 store discount coupon and issued 20,000 coupons. Based on past experience, Mega Chocolate Chip estimates that 50% of the coupons will be redeemed. The January 1, 2010, journal entry to record the coupons is as follows:

| | | | |
|---|---|---|---|
| Jan 1 | Sales Discount for Coupon Redemptions | 2,000 | |
| | Coupon Liability | | 2,000 |
| | To accrue estimated coupon liability. | | |
| | (20,000 x 50% x $0.20) | | |

When the participating stores return their customers' 5,250 coupons for the month of January 2010, Mega Chocolate Chip Company records the redemption as follows:

| | | | |
|---|---|---|---|
| Jan 31 | Coupon Liability | 1,050 | |
| | Cash | | 1,050 |
| | To record paying grocery stores for coupons redeemed. | | |
| | (5,250 x $0.20) | | |

Sales Discount for Coupon Redemptions is a contra sales account.  Coupon Liability is a current liability on the balance sheet.

# Contingencies

study objective 3

Account for contingencies.

A contingency is an existing condition or situation that is uncertain. It is not known whether the result from the situation would be a gain or a loss until one or more events happen or do not happen. A gain will result in a related contingent asset and a loss in a related contingent liability. Both contingent assets and contingent liabilities as well as required accounting disclosure will be discussed in this chapter.

## Contingent Liabilities

Contingent liabilities are liabilities that depend on the occurrence or non-occurrence of a future event. When the future event occurs, it will confirm the existence of the liability, the amount payable, the payee, and/or the date of the payment.

For example: If a company is sued by a customer for $500,000, the amount the company will have to pay depends on a court decision that would only be known if and when a judge decides that the company owes the customer and how much it owes. If the judge decides in the company's favour, the company would owe the customer nothing. The company's liability is contingent on the judge's decision—a future event.

A contingent liability is recorded by a debit to an expense (loss) account and a credit to a liability account if both of the following conditions are met:
1. The contingency is likely to occur, and
2. the amount of the contingency can be reasonably estimated.

Examples of contingent liabilities include lawsuits, loan guarantees, threat of expropriation, and similar unusual situations. Contingent liabilities are not for ongoing and recurring activities such as product warranties.

It is necessary to disclose contingencies in the notes to the financial statements. A disclosure should be made:
- when the contingency is likely but cannot be reasonably estimated.
- if the contingency is not determinable—neither likely nor unlikely.

Even when the contingency is unlikely, it should still be disclosed when the event could have a substantial negative effect on the company's financial position.

### Contingent Assets

Contingent assets also involve uncertainty that relates to future events that may or may not occur. They are never recorded or accrued in the financial statements. They are disclosed in the notes to the financial statements only if it is likely that a gain will be realized.

Contingent liabilities and contingent assets are disclosed and recorded as follows:

| Conditions | Contingent Liability (Loss) | | Contingent Asset (Gain) | |
|---|---|---|---|---|
| | Accrue | Disclose | Accrue | Disclose |
| Likely and reasonably estimable | X | | | X |
| Likely but not estimable | | | X | X |
| Neither likely nor unlikely (not determinable) | | X | | |
| Unlikely but negative effect possible | | X | | |

# Financial Statement Presentation

Current liabilities are the first category reported in the liabilities section of the balance sheet. Each of the main types of current liabilities is listed separately. Current liabilities are usually listed in order of liquidity by maturity date; however, many companies, as a matter of custom, show bank loans, notes payable, and accounts payable first, regardless of amount.

**study objective 4**

Prepare the current liabilities section of the balance sheet.

# Appendix 10A – Payroll Accounting

Payroll accounting involves all salaries and wages paid to employees, and having payroll records for each employee. Companies are required by law to keep records for all employees and to report and remit payroll deductions with respect to provincial and federal law on employee compensation.

**study objective 5**

Calculate the payroll for a pay period (Appendix 10A).

### Employee Payroll Costs

Determining payroll costs for employees involves calculating (1) gross earnings, (2) payroll deductions, and (3) net pay.

### Gross Pay

Gross pay is the total compensation earned by an employee. It consists of wages or salaries, plus any bonuses and commissions.

Total wages are determined by multiplying the hours worked by the hourly rate of pay. Most companies are required to pay a minimum of one and one-half times the regular hourly rate for overtime hours worked. The number of hours worked before overtime is payable varies by industry and occupation.

Salary is based on a weekly, biweekly, monthly, or yearly rate. Most executive and administrative positions are salaried and do not earn overtime pay.

### Payroll Deductions

Total payroll deductions is the difference between gross pay and amount the employee actually receives. It is not an expense to the employer. The employer withholds the deduction and later pays it to the government and other agencies. Deductions may be mandatory (required by law) or voluntary (requested by the employee). Mandatory payroll deductions consist of Canada Pension Plan (CPP) contributions, Employment Insurance (EI) premiums, and personal income tax.

**Mandatory Payroll Deductions** are those deductions required by provincial and/or federal law. They include income tax, Canada Pension Plan contributions, and employment insurance premiums.

**Personal Income Tax.** Employers must withhold income tax from employees each pay period in accordance with the Income Tax Act. The amount is determined by three variables: (1) the employee's gross earnings, (2) the number of credits claimed by the employee, and (3) the length of the pay period.

There is no limit to the amount of gross pay that is subject to income tax withholdings. The higher the earnings, the higher the amount of taxes withheld. The best way to determine the amount of taxes that should be withheld is to use the payroll deduction tables supplied by the Canada Revenue Agency (CRA).

**Canada Pension Plan (CPP).** All employees between the ages of 18 and 70, whether self-employed or employed by others, must contribute to the CPP. Employees in Quebec contribute to the Quebec Pension Plan (QPP). Both plans give disability, retirement, and death benefits to qualifying Canadians.

Contribution rates are set by the federal government and are adjusted every January if there is an increase in the cost of living. At present, CPP contributions are 4.95% of pensionable earnings to a maximum earnings ceiling of $42,100 in 2006. Pensionable earnings are gross earnings less a basic yearly exemption ($3,500 in 2006).

**Employment Insurance (EI).** Only those who are employed by others pay employment insurance. Self-employed people are exempt. Employment insurance provides protection for a limited time period to employees who are temporarily laid off, who are on parental leave, or who lose their jobs.

In 2006, the Employment Insurance Act requires that employees pay a premium of 1.87% on insurable earnings to a maximum earnings ceiling of $39,000. Insurable earnings are usually gross earnings plus any taxable benefits.

**Payroll Deduction Tables.** Payroll deduction tables indicate the amount of income tax that should be withheld from gross wages, based on the number of credits claimed. The employee indicates the number of credits claimed when he/she completes a Personal Tax Credits Return (TD1). This form is required by the CRA.

Separate tables are provided for weekly, biweekly, semi-monthly, and monthly pay periods for income tax, CPP, and EI deductions. The tables provide an easy way to determine a deduction rather than calculating it. The amounts withheld for these deductions vary by wage level and different pay periods. Tables are provided in hard copy by the CRA, but can be downloaded from the CRA's website.

**Voluntary Payroll Deductions.** Employees may authorize withholdings for charitable, retirement, and other purposes. The employee must authorize these voluntary withholdings from gross earnings in writing. Deductions for union dues, extended health insurance, life insurance, and pension plans are often made in a group basis, while charitable deductions like the United Way are done individually.

**Net Pay.** Net pay is calculated as follows:
> Gross earnings - Payroll deductions = Net pay.

## Employer Payroll Costs

In addition to the initial expense for the total payroll (Wages and Salaries Expense) there are additional employer payroll costs. The federal government requires CPP and EI contributions from employers. The provincial governments requires employer funding of workplace health, safety, and compensation plans.

### Canada Pension Plan
Employers must match each employee's CPP contribution with an equal amount. The matching contribution results in an employee benefits expense for the employer. The liability is CPP Payable.

### Employment Insurance
Employers must contribute 1.4 times the employee EI deduction. The Employee Benefits Expense is debited for this premium and the liability credited is EI Payable.

### Provincial Workplace Health, Safety, and Compensation Plans
Workplace health, safety, and compensation plans give benefits to workers who are injured or disabled on the job. Employers must contribute to the plan at a rate based on risk of injury and past experience. The cost is paid entirely by the employer—there is no employee contribution.

### Additional Employee Benefits
Employers incur other employee benefit costs for paid absences and post-employment benefits.

**Paid Absences.** Employers incur costs for employees for paid vacations, sick pay benefits, and paid holidays. Employees have the right to receive compensation for absences under certain conditions. When the liability for future paid absences can be estimated, it should be accrued. When it cannot be estimated, it should be disclosed in notes to the statements.

**Post-Employment Benefits.** Post employment benefits are payments by employers to retired or terminated employees. These payments are for supplemental health and dental care, life insurance, and pensions.

### Recording the Payroll

Recording the payroll involves maintaining payroll records, recording payroll expenses and liabilities, paying the payroll, and filing and remitting payroll deductions.

### Payroll Records

Separate earnings records are kept for each employee and updated after each pay period. The employee earnings record provides a cumulative record of each employee's gross earnings, deductions, and net pay during the year. The employer uses this record to determine when an employee has reached the maximum earnings subject to CPP and EI premiums.

In addition to employee earnings records, many companies prepare a payroll register in which gross pay, deductions, and net pay per employee for each period are recorded. In other companies, the payroll register is a supplementary record that gives the data for a general journal entry and later posting to the ledger accounts.

### Recognizing Payroll Expenses and Liabilities

Payroll costs are incurred for employees' gross salaries and wages and the employer contributions. Employee payroll deductions are collected by the employer and paid to the government or another third party. The deductions remain a current liability to the company until they are paid.

### Employee Payroll Costs.

The typical journal entry to record a payroll is as follows:

| | | |
|---|---|---|
| Salaries Expense | XXX | |
| Wages Expense | XXX | |
|     CPP Payable | | XXX |
|     EI Payable | | XXX |
|     Income Tax Payable | | XXX |
|     United Way Payable | | XXX |
|     Union Dues Payable | | XXX |
|     Salaries and Wages Payable | | XXX |

**Employer Payroll Costs.** Employer payroll costs include the matching amounts for CPP and EI, and the employers' amounts for workers' compensation plans and vacation pay. There may be other costs, like health tax levied in Ontario, that would increase employer payroll costs.

The typical entry for recording payroll costs is as follows:

| | | |
|---|---|---|
| Employee Benefits Expense | XXX | |
|     CPP Payable | | XXX |
|     EI Payable | | XXX |
|     Workers' Compensation Payable | | XXX |
|     Vacation Pay Payable | | XXX |

The liabilities are current liabilities since they will be paid within the next year. Employee Benefits Expense are sometimes combined with Salaries and Wages Expense on the income statement and are classified as operating expenses of the company.

**Recording Payment of the Payroll**

Payment of the payroll may be made by cheque or by electronic transfer of funds from the employer's bank account to the employee's bank account. A statement of earnings document that shows the employee's gross earnings, payroll deductions, and net pay must accompany the cheques, or given to the employee if the transfer is done electronically.

The entry to record the payroll payment is as follows:

| | | |
|---|---|---|
| Salaries and Wages Payable | XXX | |
| Cash | | XXX |

When companies report and remit their payroll deductions, they combine withholdings of income tax, CPP, and EI.  Income tax, CPP, and EI must be reported and remitted monthly to the CRA on a Statement of Account for Current Source Deductions (Form PD7A) on or before the 15th day of the month following the payroll period.

Provincial workplace health, safety and compensation plans require payments to be remitted regularly.  When payroll deductions are remitted, the accounting entry is as follows:

| | | |
|---|---|---|
| CPP Payable | XXX | |
| EI Payable | XXX | |
| Income Tax Payable | XXX | |
| United Way Payable | XXX | |
| Union Dues Payable | XXX | |
| Workers' Compensation Payable | XXX | |
| *Cash | | XXX |

*This cash payment is not a single cheque. CPP, EI and Income Tax are paid to the government. United Way, union dues and Workers' Compensation would be three separate cheques to different authorities.

At the end of each calendar year, a statement showing gross earnings, all payroll deductions, and income tax withheld for the year for each employee earnings is prepared.  This information is reported to the CRA by the last day of February of the year following.  The employer is required to provide each employee with a Statement of Remuneration Paid (Form T4) by the same date.

# Demonstration Problem (SO 1 and 2)

The following are selected transactions of the Cascade Costume Company during February and March 2009:

Feb. 10    Sales on credit for the period Feb. 1–10 totaled $100,000. 6% GST and 8% PST were added to sales.

Feb. 16    Based on experience, it is estimated that cost of the product warranty liability will be approximately 5% of the sales for the month. The company sets up the liability for warranty expense. The company expects total sales for the month to be $300,000.

Feb. 18    Items under warranty were repaired. Costs for labour and repair parts were in the amount of $300.

Feb. 28    Wages to four new employees in the amount of $2,600 were calculated to February 28. The total amounts withheld were; Income tax $425.00, CPP $116.50, and EI $48.62. The company's matched contributions were for CPP (1 times) and EI (1.4 times). The employer benefit costs also were recorded.

Feb. 28    Wages were paid to employees.

Feb. 28    A $15,000, 2-month, 10% note payable signed on December 31, 2008, was paid off. Interest had been accrued to January 31, 2008.

Mar. 15    Withholdings from employees were paid to the government agency.

## Solution to Demonstration Problem

| General Journal | | | JI |
|---|---|---|---|
| **Date** | **Account Titles and Explanation** | **Debit** | **Credit** |
| 2009 | | | |
| Feb.   10 | Accounts Receivable | 114,000.00 | |
| | GST Payable | | 6,000.00 |
| | PST Payable | | 8,000.00 |
| | Sales | | 100,000.00 |
| | To record sales and sales taxes payable. | | |
| 16 | Warranty Expense | 15,000.00 | |
| | Warranty Liability | | 15,000.00 |
| | To accrue estimated warranty costs. | | |
| | ($300,000 × 5%) | | |
| | | | |
| 18 | Warranty Liability | 300.00 | |
| | Repair Parts Inventory, Wages Payable | | 300.00 |
| | To honour warranty contracts to date. | | |
| | | | |
| 28 | Wages Expense | 2,600.00 | |
| | Income Tax Payable | | 425.00 |
| | CPP Payable | | 116.50 |
| | EI Payable | | 48.62 |
| | Wages Payable | | 2,009.88 |
| | To record wages payable. | | |
| | | | |
| | Employee Benefits Expense | 184.57 | |
| | CPP Payable | | 116.50 |
| | EI Payable | | 68.07 |
| | To record employee benefit costs to date. | | |
| | | | |
| 28 | Wages Payable | 2,009.88 | |
| | Cash | | 2,009.88 |
| | To record payment of wages. | | |

| General Journal | | | J1 |
|---|---|---|---|
| **Date** | **Account Titles and Explanation** | **Debit** | **Credit** |
| 28 | Note Payable | 15,000.00 | |
| | Interest Payable | 125.00 | |
| | Interest Expense | 125.00 | |
| | Cash | | 15,250.00 |
| | To record payment of Note Payable with accrued interest and current interest expense. | | |
| | | | |
| Mar. 15 | Income Tax Payable | 425.00 | |
| | CPP Payable | 233.00 | |
| | EI Payable | 116.69 | |
| | Cash | | 774.69 |
| | To record payment of withholdings and employee benefit costs. | | |

# Review Questions and Exercises

## Multiple Choice

Circle the letter that best answers each of the following statements.

1. (SO 1) Which of the following statements concerning current liabilities is incorrect?

   a.  A current liability occurs as a result of accrued interest.

   b.  A company that has more current liabilities than current assets is usually the subject of some concern.

   c.  Current liabilities include prepaid expenses.

   d.  A current liability is a debt that can reasonably be expected to be paid out of existing current assets or that results in the creation of other current liabilities.

Questions 2 and 3 pertain to the following information:

On October 1, 2010, DeHaviland Company issued a $28,000, 9-month, 10% note.

2. (SO 1) If the DeHaviland Company is preparing financial statements at December 31, 2010, the adjusting entry for accrued interest will include:

   a.  credit to Notes Payable of $700.

   b.  debit to Interest Expense of $700.

   c.  credit to Interest Payable of $2,100.

   d.  debit to Interest Expense of $2,800.

3. (SO 1) Assuming interest was accrued on June 30, 2011, the entry to record the payment of the note will include a:

   a.  debit to Interest Expense of $700.

   b.  credit to Cash of $28,000.

   c.  debit to Interest Payable of $2,100.

   d.  debit to Notes Payable of $30,100.

4. (SO 1) On August 1, 2010, a company borrowed cash and signed a one-year, interest-bearing note that matures on August 1, 2011. How will the note payable and the related interest be classified in the December 31, 2010, balance sheet?

   |     | Note Payable | Interest Payable |
   | --- | --- | --- |
   | a.  | Current liability | Non-current liability |
   | b.  | Non-current liability | Current liability |
   | c.  | Current liability | Current liability |
   | d.  | Long-term liability | Not shown |

5. (SO 1) Travis Company has total proceeds from sales, including GST, of $21,200. If the GST is 6%, the amount to be credited to the account Sales is:

   a.  $21,000.

   b.  $19,900.

   c.  $19,000.

   d.  $20,000.

6. (SO 1) An operating line of credit has the following features except:

   a.  it is pre-authorized by the bank.
   b.  it helps companies manage temporary cash shortfalls.
   c.  it does not have a pre-set limit.
   d.  it enables timely payments of current liabilities.

7. (SO 1)   Money borrowed through a line of credit:

   a.  is normally borrowed on a short-term basis.
   b.  is repayable at any time when the company has money.
   c.  covers any and all cheques written by the company.
   d.  is usually demanded by the bank without notice.


Using the following information, answer Questions 8 and 9:

During 2010, Preston Company sells 1,200 products at $10 each. The products are sold with a one-year warranty. Preston estimates that 12% of the units sold will be returned under warranty and repaired at an average cost of $3 per unit. During 2010, 108 units are repaired under warranty at an average cost of $3 per unit. The balance in Preston Company's Warranty Liability account at January 1, 2010, is $380 (credit).

8. (SO 2) The amount of warranty expense that Preston Company should report for 2010 is:

   a.  $1,440.
   b.  $144.
   c.  $324.
   d.  $432.

9. (SO 2) The balance in the warranty liability account at December 31, 2010, is:

   a.  $380.
   b.  $488.
   c.  $1,136.
   d.  $704.

10. (SO 2) All of the following statements about promotions are true except:

   a.  companies offer promotions to attract and keep customers.
   b.  companies expect promotions will increase sales
   c.  promotions result in an estimated liability.
   d.  promotions are recorded as an increase in expense.

11. (SO 2) In September 2009, the Lucky Company issued 1,000,000 store discount coupons which would save customers $0.50 on each Wonder Toy purchased.  The company estimates that 10% of the coupons would be redeemed when the promotion expires on January 31, 2010.   By December 31, 2009, 40,000 coupons had been redeemed.  The balance in the account Coupon Liability is:

   a.  $10,000.
   b.  $60,000.
   c.  $30,000.
   d.  $40,000.

12. (SO 3) How should a contingent loss be handled if it is reasonably likely and the amount can be reasonably estimated?

| | **Accrued** | **Disclosed** |
|---|---|---|
| a. | Yes | No |
| b. | No | Yes |
| c. | Yes | Yes |
| d. | No | No |

13. (SO 3) A contingent loss need not be recorded or disclosed when:

    a. it is likely the contingency will happen and the amount can be reasonably estimated.
    b. it is likely the contingency will happen but the amount cannot be reasonably estimated.
    c. it is not determinable if the contingency will happen and the amount cannot be reasonably estimated.
    d. it is very unlikely that the contingency will happen.

14. (SO 3) A contingent loss for which the amount can be reasonably estimated should be recorded when the outcome of the contingency is:

    a. likely.
    b. unlikely.
    c. negative.
    d. desirable.

15. (SO 3) All of the following statements about contingent assets are true except:

    a. they involve uncertainty that will be resolved in the future.
    b. an example is a legal action that could favour the company.
    c. they are never recorded or accrued in the financial statements.
    d. they are never disclosed under any circumstance.

16. (SO 3) Contingent assets are disclosed when they are likely and reasonably estimable but never recorded because:

    a. this is the same way contingent liabilities are treated.
    b. it is likely that gains may not be realized by the company.
    c. of the conservative characteristic of accounting.
    d. it is impossible to estimate the exact amount of the asset.

17. (SO 4) Which of the following would not be classified as a current liability?

    a. 6-month Note Receivable.
    b. 10-month Note Payable.
    c. Unearned Revenue.
    d. Warranty Liability.

18. (SO 4) The relationship between current liabilities and current assets is monitored by companies for all the following reasons except:

    a. it measures working capital by subtracting current liabilities from current assets.
    b. it provides information about the short-term ability of the company to pay debt.
    c. it lets the company know if it will be able to make current payments.
    d. it measures the current ratio by dividing the current liabilities by the current assets.

19. (SO 5) The department responsible for paying payroll is the:

    a. controller's department.

    b. human resources department.

    c. timekeeping department.

    d. payroll department.

20. (SO 5) The department responsible for maintaining employee earnings records in accordance with provincial and federal laws is the:

    a. controller's department.

    b. human resources department.

    c. timekeeping department.

    d. payroll department.

21. (SO 5) Jan Turner earns $16 per hour for a 40-hour work week and $24 per hour for overtime work. If Turner works 44 hours, and overtime payment is 1.5 times regular hourly wages, her gross earnings are:

    a. $704.

    b. $736.

    c. $836.

    d. $1,056.

22. (SO 5) Lewis Latimer, an employee of Southam Company, has gross earnings for the month of October of $4,000. CPP is 4.95% of gross earnings, EI premium is 1.87% of gross earnings, income tax amounts to $1,072 for the month, and Lewis authorizes voluntary deductions of $10 per month to the United Way. The company must match the CPP deduction and pay 1.4 times the EI premium. What is the net pay for Lewis Latimer?

    a. $2,447.20

    b. $2,342.80

    c. $2,645.20

    d. $2,918.00

23. (SO 5) The journal entry to record the payroll for Garvey Company for the week ending January 8, would probably include a:

    a. credit to Office Salaries.

    b. credit to Wages Expense.

    c. debit to Income Tax Payable.

    d. credit to CPP Payable.

24. (SO 5) The journal entry for Hansberry Corporation to record employer payroll costs will include a:

    a. debit to Wages Expense.

    b. debit to EI Payable.

    c. debit to Income Taxes Payable.

    d. debit to Employee Benefits Expense.

25. (SO 5) The document that provides a cumulative summary of each employee's gross earnings, payroll deductions, and net pay during the year and is required to be maintained by federal law is the:

    a.  payroll register.
    b.  employee earnings record.
    c.  statement of remuneration paid.
    d.  approved time cards.

## Matching

Match each term with its definition by writing the appropriate letter in the space provided.

| **Terms** | **Definitions** |
|---|---|
| _____ 1. Earnings record | a. Payments made by an employer, in addition to wages and salaries, to give pension, insurance, medical, or other benefits to its employees. |
| _____ 2. Notes Payable | b. Deductions required by law and include income tax, Canada Pension Plan contributions and employment insurance premiums. |
| _____ 3. Contingent liability | c. A record kept and updated after each pay period for each employee by an employer. It accumulates gross pay, deductions and net pay of each employee. |
| _____ 4. Employee benefits | d. Promises made by the seller to a buyer to repair or replace a product if it is defective or does not perform as intended. |
| _____ 5. Contingency | e. A potential liability that may become an actual liability in the future. |
| _____ 6. Mandatory payroll deductions | f. Amounts withheld from gross pay to determine the amount of net pay due to an employee. |
| _____ 7. Product Warranties | g. An existing condition or situation that is uncertain and could lead to a loss and the result would only be known when one or more future events happened or do not happen. |
| _____ 8. Operating line of credit | h. Obligations in the form of written promissory notes. |
| _____ 9. Property taxes | i. Cash rebates, coupons, or other items offered as a decrease in sales price to encourage sales. |
| _____ 10. Gross pay | |
| _____ 11. Promotions | |

_____ 12. Payroll deductions

j.  Total compensation earned by an employee.

k.  Pre-authorized approval to borrow money at a bank when it is needed, up to a pre-set limit.

l.  Taxes charged by the municipal and provincial governments and are calculated at a specified rate for every $100 of assessed value of property.

## Exercises

**E10-1**    (SO 1) The following transactions took place during 2010 for Reel Pots and Pans Company:

Aug.  1    Borrowed $10,000 cash from the Hong Kong Bank by issuing a $10,000, 8-month, 9% note. Interest is payable at maturity.

Oct.  1    Borrowed $18,000 cash from the First Financial Credit Union by issuing a 3-month, 10% note. Interest is payable the first of each month starting November 1.

Nov.  1    Paid one month's interest on the October 1 note.

Dec.  1    Paid one month's interest on the October 1 note.

Dec.  24    Determined from cash register readings that sales were $27,360 with the GST(6%) and PST(8%) included.

### Instructions
(a)  Journalize the transactions above.
(b)  Prepare the adjusting entries for the two notes at December 31, 2010.
(c)  Record the payment of the two notes in 2011 at their maturity dates.

| | General Journal | | JI |
|---|---|---|---|
| **Date** | **Account Titles and Explanation** | **Debit** | **Credit** |
| 2010 | | | |
| (a) | | | |
| | | | |
| | | | |
| | | | |
| | | | |
| | | | |
| | | | |
| | | | |
| | | | |
| | | | |
| | | | |
| | | | |
| | | | |
| | | | |
| | | | |
| | | | |
| | | | |
| | | | |
| | | | |
| | | | |
| | | | |
| | | | |
| | | | |
| | | | |
| | | | |
| | | | |
| | | | |
| | | | |
| | | | |
| | | | |
| | | | |
| | | | |

| General Journal | | | J1 |
|---|---|---|---|
| **Date** | **Account Titles and Explanation** | **Debit** | **Credit** |
| 2010 | | | |
| (b) | | | |
| | | | |
| | | | |
| | | | |
| | | | |
| | | | |
| | | | |
| | | | |
| | | | |
| | | | |
| | | | |
| | | | |
| (c) | | | |
| | | | |
| | | | |
| | | | |
| | | | |
| | | | |
| | | | |
| | | | |
| | | | |
| | | | |
| | | | |
| | | | |
| | | | |
| | | | |
| | | | |

**E10-2** (SO 1) Coast Industries received its annual property tax bill for $22,200 on May 1, payable June 30. Coast has a December 31 fiscal year end and makes annual adjusting entries.

## Instructions

(a) Prepare the journal entry to record the receipt of the property tax bill on May 1.
(b) Prepare the journal entry to record the payment of the property tax bill June 30.
(c) Prepare any adjusting entries required at December 31.

| | General Journal | | JI |
|---|---|---|---|
| **Date** | **Account Titles and Explanation** | **Debit** | **Credit** |
| 2009 | | | |
| (a) | | | |
| | | | |
| | | | |
| | | | |
| | | | |
| | | | |
| (b) | | | |
| | | | |
| | | | |
| | | | |
| | | | |
| (c) | | | |
| | | | |
| | | | |
| | | | |
| | | | |
| | | | |

**E10-3**    (SO 2) Robins Wireless sells cell phones with a 120-day warranty for defective merchandise. Based on past experience Robins estimates 2% of the units sold will become defective in the warranty period. Management estimates that repair costs will average $20 per unit. The units sold and actual units defective in the first two months of 2009 are as follows:

| Month | Units Sold | Units Defective | Actual Repair Cost |
|-------|------------|-----------------|--------------------|
| January | 15,000 | 150 | $3,000 |
| February | 16,000 | 210 | $4,200 |

Instructions

(a) Prepare journal entries to record the estimated liability costs on January 31, and February 28.

(b) Prepare journal entries to record the repairing the defective units.

| General Journal | | | JI |
|-----------------|---|---|----|
| **Date** | **Account Titles and Explanation** | **Debit** | **Credit** |
| 2009 | | | |
| (a) | | | |
| | | | |
| | | | |
| | | | |
| | | | |
| | | | |
| | | | |
| | | | |
| | | | |
| (b) | | | |
| | | | |
| | | | |
| | | | |
| | | | |
| | | | |
| | | | |
| | | | |

**E10-4**    (SO 2) In September 2009 Beautique Skin Care Company sold 10,000 packages of its newly formulated skin cleanser. Each package included a $4 mail-in rebate form if the consumer sends in proof of purchase with the completed rebate form. Beautique estimates that 20% of the purchasers will claim the rebate. By December 31, 2009, 1,500 customers had been issued their rebate.

**Instructions**
(a)  Prepare an entry to record the estimated rebate liability as of September 30, 2009.
(b)  Prepare an entry to record issuing the rebates redeemed by end of December 31, 2009.

| | General Journal | | J1 |
|---|---|---|---|
| **Date** | **Account Titles and Explanation** | **Debit** | **Credit** |
| 2009 | | | |
| (a) | | | |
| | | | |
| | | | |
| | | | |
| | | | |
| | | | |
| (b) | | | |
| | | | |
| | | | |
| | | | |
| | | | |
| | | | |

**\*E10-5** (SO 5) The following information pertains to the payroll of B. T. MacDonald Company for the week ended January 24, 2010. All hours over 44 are paid at one and one-half times the regular hourly rate.

| Employee | Total Hours Worked | Hourly Rate | Income Tax | United Way | Union Dues |
|---|---|---|---|---|---|
| E. Bouchet | 45 | $13.00 | $110 | $10 | $5 |
| C. Cullen | 44 | 15.00 | 138 | 12 | 5 |
| M. Henson | 38 | 10.00 | 64 | 10 | 5 |
| B. Mays | 48 | 12.00 | 100 | 14 | 5 |

## Instructions

(a) Complete the schedule below. CPP is 4.95% of gross earnings, and EI is 1.87% of gross earnings.
(b) Prepare the entry to record the payroll on January 24.
(c) Prepare the journal entry to record payment of the payroll on January 26.
(d) Record the employer's payroll costs, assuming employers must match employees' CPP and pay 1.4 times the employees' EI.
(e) Record the payment of payroll withholdings to the Receiver General on February 15.

(a)

| | Gross Earnings | CPP | Employment Insurance | Income Tax | United Way | Union Dues | Net Pay |
|---|---|---|---|---|---|---|---|
| E. Bouchet | | | | | | | |
| C. Cullen | | | | | | | |
| M. Henson | | | | | | | |
| B. Mays | | | | | | | |
| Totals | | | | | | | |

| | General Journal | | JI |
|---|---|---|---|
| **Date** | **Account Titles and Explanation** | **Debit** | **Credit** |
| 2010 | | | |
| (b) | | | |
| | | | |
| | | | |
| | | | |
| | | | |
| | | | |
| | | | |
| (c) | | | |
| | | | |
| | | | |
| | | | |
| | | | |
| | | | |
| | | | |
| (d) | | | |
| | | | |
| | | | |
| | | | |
| | | | |
| (e) | | | |
| | | | |
| | | | |
| | | | |
| | | | |
| | | | |
| | | | |

# Solutions to Review Questions and Exercises

## Multiple Choice

1.  (c)  Prepaid expenses are current assets. Answers (a), (b), and (d) are all correct statements.

2.  (b)  The adjusting entry for the company is as follows:

    | | | |
    |---|---|---|
    | Interest Expense | 700 | |
    |     Interest Payable | | 700 |

    ($28,000 x 10% x 3/12)

3.  (c)  The entry to record the payment of the note is as follows:

    | | | |
    |---|---|---|
    | Notes Payable | 28,000 | |
    | Interest Payable | 2,100 | |
    |     Cash | | 30,100 |

4.  (c)  Because the note and the accrued interest are payable within one year from December 31, 2010, they should both be classified as current liabilities.

5.  (d)  The entry for Travis Company to record sales and sales taxes is as follows:

    | | | |
    |---|---|---|
    | Cash | 21,200 | |
    |     Sales ($21,200 / 106%) | | 20,000 |
    |     GST Payable ($20,000 x 6%) | | 1,200 |

6.  (c)  An operating line of credit is pre-authorized by the bank so a company can borrow money when needed up to a pre-set limit.

7.  (a)  A line of credit makes it easy for a company to borrow on a short-term basis.

8.  (d)  The amount of warranty expense to report for the year is based on the estimated number of units to be repaired (1,200 x 12% = 144), multiplied by the average estimated cost to repair each unit (144 x $3= $432).

9.  (b)  The ending balance in the estimated warranty liability account is the opening balance ($380), plus the estimated warranty expense for the year ($432), minus the actual warranty claims made during the year (108 x $3 = $324).

10. (d)  Promotions are accounted for as a decrease in revenue not as an expense.

11. (c)  The Lucky Company estimates that 100,000 coupons would be redeemed so the Coupon Liability account would have a credit balance of $50,000. The 40,000 coupons redeemed by December 2009 would be(40,000 X $0.50) $20,000 which would be credited to the account. Thus, the balance in the account would be $30,000.

12.  (c)  When a contingency is likely and the amount reasonably estimable, the liability should be recorded in the accounts. When a contingency does not meet the two conditions for accrual described above, only disclosure of the contingency is required, unless it is very unlikely, in which case no disclosure is made.

13.  (d)  If the possibility of the contingency happening is very unlikely, the liability need not be recorded or disclosed.

14.  (a)  A contingency for which the amount of loss can be reasonably estimated should be recorded when the outcome of the contingency is reasonably possible.

15.  (d)  Contingent assets (gains) are disclosed when they are likely and are reasonably estimable and also when they are likely but not estimable.

16.  (c)  The goal of conservatism is to be sure that any negative effect on investors and creditors be fully disclosed but not recorded.

17.  (a)  A 6-month Note Receivable would be classified as a current asset, not a current liability. All of the other items would normally be classified as current liabilities.

18.  (d)  is false. Companies measure the current ratio by dividing the current assets by current liabilities. The other statements are true.

19.  (a)  The controller's department should be responsible for the payment of the payroll. The other departments perform other important payroll functions but do not pay the payroll.

20.  (d)  The payroll department should be responsible for maintaining earnings records in accordance with provincial and federal laws.

21.  (a)  Gross earnings are $704. (Regular 44 x $16 = $704). Overtime premiums are not paid until the employee has worked more than 44 hours in a seven-day period.

22.  (c)  The net pay is calculated as follows:

| | | |
|---|---:|---:|
| Gross earnings | | $4,000.00 |
| Payroll deductions: | | |
| Employment Insurance ($4,000 x 1.87%) | $ 74.80 | |
| Income tax | 1,072.00 | |
| Canada Pension Plan ($4,000 x 4.95%) | 198.00 | |
| United Way | 10.00 | 1,354.80 |
| Net pay | | $2,645.20 |

23.  (d)  An example of a typical payroll entry is as follows:

| | | |
|---|---|---|
| Office Salaries Expense | XXXX | |
| Wages Expense | XXXX | |
|     CPP (or QPP) Payable | | XXXX |
|     Income Tax Payable | | XXXX |
|     EI Payable | | XXXX |
|     United Way Payable | | XXXX |
|     Salaries and Wages Payable | | XXXX |

24.  (d)  Employee benefit costs include CPP and EI withholdings that are matched by the employer and other expenses paid totally by the employer.

25.  (b)  Choices (a), (c) and (d)—the payroll register, the statement of remuneration paid and approved time cards all relate to a given pay period.

## Matching

| | | | | |
|---|---|---|---|---|
| 1. | c | | 7. | d |
| 2. | h | | 8. | k |
| 3. | e | | 9. | l |
| 4. | a | | 10. | j |
| 5. | g | | 11. | i |
| 6. | b | | 12. | f |

# Exercises

## E10-1

| | General Journal | | J1 |
|---|---|---|---|
| **Date** | **Account Titles and Explanation** | **Debit** | **Credit** |
| 2010 | | | |
| (a) | | | |
| Aug. 1 | Cash | 10,000 | |
| |     Notes Payable | | 10,000 |
| | To record issue of $10,000, 8-month, | | |
| | 9% note. | | |
| | | | |
| Oct. 1 | Cash | 18,000 | |
| |     Notes Payable | | 18,000 |
| | To record issuance of $18,000, 3-month, | | |
| | 10% note. | | |
| | | | |
| Nov. 1 | Interest Expense | 150 | |
| |     Cash | | 150 |
| | To paid one month interest on Oct. 1 note. | | |
| | ($18,000 x 10% x 1/12) | | |
| | | | |
| Dec. 1 | Interest Expense | 150 | |
| |     Cash | | 150 |
| | To paid one month interest on Oct. 1 note. | | |
| | ($18,000 x 10% x 1/12) | | |
| | | | |
| Dec. 24 | Cash | 27,360 | |
| |     Sales ($27,360 ÷ 1.14) | | 24,000 |
| |     GST Payable ($24,000 x 6%) | | 1,440 |
| |     PST Payable ($24,000 x 8%) | | 1,920 |
| | To record daily sales and sales taxes. | | |

| General Journal | | | J1 |
|---|---|---|---|
| **Date** | **Account Titles and Explanation** | **Debit** | **Credit** |
| 2010 | | | |
| (b) | | | |
| Dec.  31 | Interest Expense | 375 | |
| | Interest Payable | | 375 |
| | To record interest expense for five months ($10,000 x 9% x 5/12). | | |
| | | | |
| 31 | Interest Expense | 150 | |
| | Interest Payable | | 150 |
| | To record interest expense for 1 month ($18,000 x 10% x 1/12). | | |
| (c) | | | |
| 2011 | | | |
| Jan.  1 | Notes Payable | 18,000 | |
| | Interest Payable | 150 | |
| | Cash | | 18,150 |
| | To record payment of First Financial Credit Union note and accrued interest. | | |
| | | | |
| Mar.  31 | Interest Expense | 225 | |
| | Interest Payable | | 225 |
| | To record interest expense for 3 months ($10,000 x 9% x 3/12) | | |
| | | | |
| Mar.  31 | Notes Payable | 10,000 | |
| | Interest Payable | 600 | |
| | Cash | | 10,600 |
| | To record payment of Hong Kong bank note with accrued interest. | | |

E10-2

| General Journal | | | JI |
|---|---|---|---|
| **Date** | **Account Titles** | **Debit** | **Credit** |
| 2009 | | | |
| (a) | | | |
| May    1 | Property Tax Expense | 7,400 | |
| | Property Tax Payable | | 7,400 |
| | ($22,200 x 4/12) | | |
| | | | |
| (b) | | | |
| Jun.    30 | Property Tax Expense* | 3,700 | |
| | Property Tax Payable | 7,400 | |
| | Prepaid Property Taxes** | 11,100 | |
| | Cash | | 22,200 |
| | *($22,200 x 2/12) = $3,700 | | |
| | ** ($22,200 x 6/12) = $11,100 | | |
| | | | |
| (c) | | | |
| Dec. 31 | Property Tax Expense | 11,100 | |
| | Prepaid Property Taxes | | 11,100 |

E10-3

| General Journal | | | | J1 |
|---|---|---|---|---|
| **Date** | | **Account Titles** | **Debit** | **Credit** |
| (a) | | | | |
| Jan. | 31 | Warranty Expense | 6,000 | |
| | | Warranty Liability | | 6,000 |
| | | To accrue estimated warranty liability. | | |
| | | (15,000 x 2% x $20) | | |
| | | | | |
| Feb. | 28 | Warranty Expense | 6,400 | |
| | | Warranty Liability | | 6,400 |
| | | To accrue estimated warranty liability. | | |
| | | (16,000 x 2% x $20) | | |
| (b) | | | | |
| Jan. | 31 | Warranty Liability | 3,000 | |
| | | Repair Parts(and/or Wages Payable) | | 3,000 |
| | | To record honouring of 150 warranties. | | |
| | | | | |
| Feb. | 28 | Warranty Liability | 4,200 | |
| | | Repair Parts(and/or Wages Payable) | | 4,200 |
| | | To record honouring of 210 warranties. | | |

E10-4

| General Journal | | Debit | **JI** |
|---|---|---|---|
| **Date** | **Account Titles and Explanation** | **Debit** | **Credit** |
| (a) | | | |
| Sep.    30 | Sales Discount for Rebate Redemption | 8,000 | |
| | Rebate Liability | | 8,000 |
| | To accrue estimated rebate liability. | | |
| | (10,000 x 20% x $4) | | |
| | | | |
| (b) | | | |
| Dec.    31 | Rebate Liability | 6,000 | |
| | Cash | | 6,000 |
| | To record redemption of rebates (1,500 x $4) | | |

*E10-5

(a)

| | Gross Earnings | CPP | EI | Income Tax | United Way | Union Dues | Net Pay |
|---|---|---|---|---|---|---|---|
| E. Bouchet | $   591.50 | $29.28 | $11.06 | $110.00 | $10.00 | $ 5.00 | $   426.16 |
| C. Cullen | 660.00 | 32.67 | 12.34 | 138.00 | 12.00 | 5.00 | 459.99 |
| M. Henson | 380.00 | 18.81 | 7.11 | 64.00 | 10.00 | 5.00 | 275.08 |
| B. Mays | 600.00 | 29.70 | 11.22 | 100.00 | 14.00 | 5.00 | 440.08 |
| | $2,231.50 | $110.46 | $41.73 | $412.00 | $46.00 | $20.00 | $1,601.31 |

| General Journal | | | JI |
|---|---|---|---|
| **Date** | **Account Titles and Explanation** | **Debit** | **Credit** |
| 2010 | | | |
| (b) | | | |
| Jan. 24 | Wages Expense | 2,231.50 | |
| | CPP Payable | | 110.46 |
| | EI Payable | | 41.73 |
| | Income Tax Payable | | 412.00 |
| | United Way Payable | | 46.00 |
| | Union Dues Payable | | 20.00 |
| | Wages Payable | | 1,601.31 |
| | To record payroll for the week ending January 24. | | |
| | | | |
| (c) | | | |
| Jan. 26 | Wages Payable | 1,601.31 | |
| | Cash | | 1,601.31 |
| | To record payment of January 24 payroll. | | |
| | | | |
| (d) | | | |
| Jan. 26 | Employee Benefits Expense | 168.88 | |
| | CPP Payable | | 110.46 |
| | EI Payable | | 58.42 |
| | To record employer payroll cost on January 24. | | |
| | | | |
| (e) | | | |
| Feb. 15 | Income Tax Payable | 412.00 | |
| | CPP Payable | 220.92 | |
| | EI Payable | 100.15 | |
| | Cash | | 733.07 |
| | To record payment to the Receiver General for January payroll. | | |